DAN HOTCHKISS

Ministry
and Money

A Guide for Clergy
and Their Friends

An Alban Institute Publication

Scripture quotations, unless otherwise noted, are from the New Revised Standard Version of the Bible, copyright © 1989, Division of Christian Education of the National Council of Churches of Christ in the United States of America, and are used by permission.

The parable by the Rev. Clinton Lee Scott that opens chapter 7 is used with the kind permission of his son, the Rev. Peter Lee Scott.

Library of Congress Card Number 2002104637

ISBN 1-56699-261-3

CONTENTS

The realms of economics and religion have never been entirely separate for me. I grew up in one of those church families that are involved with every aspect of the congregation's life. My mother's choir rehearsals and my father's finance meetings were all one to me—a tithe paid from my parental budget. I came to Sunday school with money tied into the center of a handkerchief for the collection. The chime of coins exploding from their knotted prisons—each one embossed "In God We Trust"—was percussion for the offertory anthem.

A deeper connection between money and the church was made for me when I was 11 and my brother had a life-threatening and expensive motorcycle accident. Among the many kindnesses my family received from our minister and members of our congregation in the months after the accident, one stands out especially in my mind. A man who owned a small chain of APCO gas stations spoke to my father during the coffee hour after services and said, "Starting this month, you won't be getting a bill on your credit card. Let me know when you are ready, and we'll start it up again."

It is not to discount the casseroles, cards, child care, and pastor's visits we received that year that I say there was something especially significant in that gesture. Our needs were many, and the power of the personal and practical and spiritual care we received was great. But the APCO man's gesture stretched the church's care beyond its usual boundaries.

Since then, forms of religion interested only in the inner life and private virtues have to me seemed incomplete. So have congregations whose only message about money is "Give some of it to us." As I became fascinated with the world's religious history I discovered that Judaism, Christianity, and other historic traditions have had much more than that to say about how people ought to think about and use their money.

Jesus said more about money than about any other subject, or so it is often claimed (I haven't counted). If true, this claim is not surprising, given that the Torah Jesus studied says so much about the fair and generous use of money. Nor is concern with money limited to the Western traditions. Prince Gautama's struggle with the burden of inherited wealth is at the core of the Buddha's quest for enlightenment. The Prophet Muhammad received a revelation about how to know and worship God—but along with it came a code of law regulating, among other things, trade, employment, and the financial side of family life.

Even the earth's oldest scriptures, the Vedas, composed in the Indus Valley more than 3,000 years ago, describe and celebrate the sacrifice, which is one of the deeply rooted rituals of Hinduism. And what is sacrifice but making sacred the use, distribution, and relinquishment of wealth? Ritual sacrifice is one of the most widespread religious concepts; if faith is (as theologian Paul Tillich put it) "ultimate concern," then it is significant that from the earliest times we can trace, religious people have considered money a primary area of concern. Modern clergy and religious people may have reasons to compartmentalize faith from money (for one thing, it may be safer sometimes!), but as a student I found little support for doing so in the scriptures and traditions of the world.

Faith and Money: Early Explorations

When I began to think of going to seminary to become a minister, it seemed natural to think at the same time about going to business school. I had enjoyed a taste of business as president of a student housing and dining cooperative, and I wondered whether I might find a way to combine the satisfactions of the ministry with those of business leadership. The appeal of ministry for me grew mainly out of my experience in leading voluntary groups and the wish to think and write on subjects of importance. Business, on the other hand, seemed to promise possibilities to change the world in more concrete, important ways.

Closing the gap between the world of spirit and the world of money became a project for me. As a religion major, I proposed an honors project on "The Theology of Money." I suppose I had in mind something like this book. I went to my faculty advisor's office and told him I was interested in studying the ways religious people have related over the centuries to business, trade, and finance. As I spoke, I saw in his face the same glazed, faintly irritated look I had seen when he approved the mathematics courses on my schedule, or received the bill for my use of the college computer.

When I finished my sales pitch, he gave me an answer I did not forget. He answered, "No."

I continued pondering the dilemma—business school or seminary? My first preference was to be a minister of economic influence and savvy—if that was possible—or if not, to be a businessperson of religious sensibilities. I made an appointment with the minister of the church nearest the campus and told him what I was considering. I asked him, "Have you ever wished you had more knowledge about business and the world of work and money?"

He thought about this carefully, and gave an answer I did not forget. He answered, "No."

These two identical responses—one from a distinguished scholar, one from a successful pastor—taught me that relating faith and money would not be a simple task, or one that could proceed without my opposing some widespread assumptions.

Despite this discouragement, I went to seminary, but for a variety of reasons did not pursue an MBA. No one in the world of seminary studies seemed the least bit interested in whether faith and money had anything to do with one another. Seminary studies covered God, the Bible, and the spiritual life, and went from there to faith-based opinions about politics without dabbling much in economics (or other subjects that require math). I gradually forgot that I had once thought ministry and management might go together.

It seems to be a nearly universal theme in the professional lives of clergy that no matter how "practical" our seminaries try to be, we don't learn much about the "how" of leadership until we're out. I don't blame seminaries for this: most of them do well what they do best—provide an education in the literature, philosophy, and history of the faith they serve. I was lucky to attend a school that exposed students to the literature, philosophy, and history of other faiths as well. But few seminary faculty have much congregational leadership experience, and when they try to teach practical leadership, the results (with rare exceptions) range from unimpressive to ridiculous.

Even if seminaries somehow solved this problem (and most try hard), there is a more important obstacle to teaching practical skills in seminaries:

Few seminary students want to hear about them. This is the widespread observation of practicing clergy, consultants, and denominational officials who address seminary audiences. The institutional realities that to these outsiders are facts of life are of no interest to the majority of seminary students, who have yet to encounter them firsthand.

Money is one of those facts of life, and I learned about ministry and money when most seminarians do—after I had graduated.

Introduction to Ministry and Money

My first lesson came when I was barely 25 and a candidate for my first pulpit, in Boca Raton, Florida. During "candidating week"—a scratch 'n' sniff time customary in my denomination—my wife and I went to visit the former wife of the previous minister. Let's call her Emily. She had survived a messy, public divorce in which the congregation, by and large, took Emily's side. She and the children stayed; her husband left. I knew Emily already as a member of the ministerial search committee, but this was my first visit to her home.

Emily welcomed us to a typical small south-Florida house: concrete block, no basement, windows of louvered glass. The living room was small but comfortable, the furniture old but adequate.

We talked about Emily's children and the search process. Moving a little closer in the circling way of new acquaintances, we talked about the ministry. She spoke a bit about the residue of feeling in the church about her former husband, and about her as his former wife. She reassured my wife (who needed to be reassured) that the congregation would be welcoming to her, and not demanding.

Finally, she came to the point: "I wanted you to come here so you'd see how I live. I knew you'd spend most of your time this week in the bigger homes. I've found it difficult to live here among people with so much. They're wonderful people, but they just assume; they don't see anything the matter with their minister living on so little when they have so much.

"So I wanted you to see my little house and my second-hand furniture. I just thought you should know."

By now she was crying. "I'm not poor. I have about as much as I grew up with. But when you socialize on Sunday and on other days with—

some of them are literally millionaires—it makes you dissatisfied. And when you hear the way they argue about whether he should get a raise of 2 percent or 3 percent, it makes you angry. I hope it will go better for you." She wiped her cheeks and forced a smile. "I'm sure it will. You'll have a second income. It'll be better."

Her face showed a determination that reminded me—I couldn't block the image—of Scarlett O'Hara in *Gone with the Wind* saying, "As God is my witness. . . . I'll never be hungry again!" Subsequent events confirmed that association. I had the pleasure of presiding at Emily's second wedding, this time to a well-paid engineer. By then she had advanced to a fair salary herself.

Boca Raton is an exceptional community. In Boca, you see more than one Rolls Royce per day, and within a half-hour's drive of the city are squalid camps where migrant sugar workers live. Most of the residents are in between; they work at IBM, Florida Atlantic University, the public schools. But nowhere else in the United States is wealth more openly displayed. Everyone in Boca is reminded daily of his or her place in the economic pecking order. It is a harder place than most to be a poorly paid clergy leader.

But in all kinds of communities, clergy are paid salaries well below the norm for the congregations they serve. Most of the clergy families I know live on less than the people they serve would find acceptable—or they would if they depended only on the minister's salary. Ours is a society that expresses its respect for jobs by assigning them a compensation level. It is not a statement of respect for a congregation to set its clergy leader's compensation lower than what most members of the congregation would expect to earn at a similar career stage. In a culture in which every institution ranks its employees in a strict hierarchy by salary, it can be demoralizing to clergy leaders to be compensated, as some are, in the 10th or 20th percentile of the congregation.

One time-honored evasion of this problem is for clergy to marry or inherit wealth, so they can rise "above" concerns about their salary. The two-career family is a modern version of this dodge; many clergy today are married to spouses who make more money than they do. There's nothing wrong with that, except that it puts clergy in a doubly dependent situation, relying on both spouse and congregation. One consequence for congregations is that it can be difficult to attract the leader of their choice. Even when the match is good, the clergy family may not feel that it can give up a higher-paying job in favor of a lower-income calling.

Money confers independence. All clergy serve at least two masters—the faith and those who control the purse strings. This situation creates dilemmas for all clergy when the will of the largest givers conflicts with what the clergy believe is right. Such dilemmas feel especially crushing to those clergy who, between high debt and low salaries, live two or three paychecks from bankruptcy. Ideally a prophet would rely on faith alone, but I have noticed that many of the most effective religious leaders in our history, including John Cotton, Brigham Young, Mary Baker Eddy, Jane Addams, Carrie Nation, Dorothy Day, and Martin Luther King, were sound financial planners. Each of them had a reasonably secure personal financial situation based on some combination of assets, income, and expenditure control. These men and women of faith arranged their affairs to buffer their own standard of living against the slings and arrows of the world. I suspect that their financial security was one source of their courage.

What Clergy Need to Learn

It is not simply, or even mainly, low clergy salaries that moved me to write this book. Lack of money is a problem for the clergy, but a bigger problem is our lack of knowledge, skill, and confidence to give effective leadership on money issues. With many laudable exceptions, clergy do not know what they need to know to provide pastoral care to people with financial problems, to guide congregations to use money to fulfill their religious purposes, or to give leadership on moral issues involving money. Since (by my estimate) 100 percent of moral issues do involve money, a book seemed worth the effort.

It is not simply that we lack the knowledge a business leader or economist would have. As clergy we lack knowledge proper to our own role—knowledge about money as a spiritual issue in the lives of those we serve. Alban Institute founder Loren Mead wrote:

> Clergy need a kind of education we do not yet have. A friend put it this way: "Perhaps what we need is a new kind of therapy for clergy." In this area we badly need our clergy to be effective leaders; but they are not, on the whole, motivated to do things differently until a crisis arrives. Clergy do not need "head" knowledge but "heart" learning. They need to understand the

emotional impact of money in their own lives and the lives of others. They need to know why they feel uncomfortable talking about money when Jesus talked about it more than any other topic . . . he is recorded as having talked about."[1]

We clergy do, many of us, back away from talking about money, and when we try to do so, our vocabulary is inadequate to bridge the gap between what our traditions have to say and the ways members of our congregations think. It is easy to retreat into a religious gobbledygook that speaks only to the initiated. Even when what we try to say reflects the teachings of our faith, it can be too detached from everyday ideas to influence everyday people. Too much of the time, we are not preaching even to the choir.

That situation moved me to write this book. I want to challenge some of our personal and cultural assumptions about money and wealth, and what they have to do with congregations and their leaders. I write for my clergy colleagues in particular and for our spouses and our friends: I want to encourage, teach, harangue, prod, and exhort us to move past our limited relationship with money. I want us to be better stewards of our personal finances than we are. I want us to become more fluent in the economic and financial language spoken outside congregations—and increasingly inside them too. With a sounder personal foundation I want us to be more self-confident in asking for money for ourselves and for our congregations, and in asking people to consider changing how they handle money in their households and at work.

Acknowledgments

As a first-time author, I am learning that what authors say in prefaces is not a joke: I could not have done it by myself. On the most practical level, I am grateful to the Lilly Endowment, whose funding for the Alban Institute to undertake the Faith and Money project incidentally funded me to write this book. To Ian Evison, Alban's director of research, I am indebted for his confidence and help. And to Beth Ann Gaede, thanks for being coach, taskmistress, cheerleader, and editor to this not-always-cooperative writer.

More personally, I want to acknowledge a huge debt to my late father, Del, a lifelong economics major and impassioned Unitarian, and to my mother, Kay, who after some 60 years as a church musician knows more about ministers than I hope ever to know; and to the extraordinary family they launched.

To my dear friend Fran Lightsom, who listened and advised over the years as I absorbed challenging lessons about congregations, I owe much. My daughter, Carolyn, who will no doubt become an author earlier in life than I did, has read and criticized many of the words you are about to read. Meanwhile my son, Sam, provided movie breaks and a profusion of blues riffs to keep my mind from sinking in the sands of church administration.

Finally, for marrying me despite the fact that I was working on a book, for proving, by making a clergy spouse of me, that there is justice in the world, and for so many other more-or-less amazing graces, I am grateful and much more than grateful to Laurie Bilyeu Hotchkiss.

CHAPTER 1

Money in American Culture

*One's sense of the proprieties is readily offended by too
detailed and intimate a handling of industrial or other purely
human questions at the hands of the clergy. . . . These matters
that are of human and secular consequence simply, should
properly be handled with such a degree of generality and
aloofness as may imply that the speaker represents a master
whose interest in secular affairs goes only so far as to
permissively countenance them.*

Thorstein Veblen
The Theory of the Leisure Class

Our culture is deeply ambivalent about money.[1] Money is a potent
symbol of salvation for us: we spend $37 billion on state lotteries in
the hope of sudden wealth.[2] At the same time, we suspect that
there is something dangerous and evil about money: we know lottery winners'
lives are sometimes destroyed by sudden wealth, and we are strangely
comforted by watching news reports about those winners on TV. Americans
who belong to religious congregations, surveys show, do not differ much
from unaffiliated people in their attitudes toward money. Certainly religious
people share much of the ambivalence of the society at large. Before looking
at the special difficulties congregations have, let's look at the broader social
and historical context of money in American culture.

Whose American Culture?

Of course "American culture" means different things to different people. The culture of the United States is diverse and grows more diverse by the day. It is no longer valid, if it ever was, to assume that all Americans share a single civic or religious story. Immigrant groups do not always cast off their origins in favor of the mythic nationality that flows from Pilgrim fathers, Bunker Hill, and Appomattox, through the triumphs of the two world wars, across the green lawns of the Eisenhower era to the 21st century. The white, Anglo-Saxon "Protestant Establishment" of Adamses and Eliots, Roosevelts and Tafts still exists,[3] but since the 19th century this older upper class has had to share leadership with Catholics and Jews and, more recently, with Americans of African, Hispanic, and Asian heritage. Nonetheless, new leaders tend to adopt the mores of their predecessors, and so the old establishment retains a disproportionate cultural influence on American society as a whole.

As attractive as it is to define ourselves strictly by our unique cultural heritage, we all participate in a larger whole as well; the tension is neither comfortable nor avoidable. "The pluribus," as historian Wilfred M. McClay has put it, "remains in symbiosis with the unum."[4]

As a person of mostly Anglo-Saxon origins, my struggle is to resist a self-deception in which my ethnic culture and the broader one conspire— namely the belief that "American" and "Anglo-American" are the same thing. I am continually tempted to deny this struggle by believing I have outgrown the self-deception, but once in a while some incident unmasks my illusions. Several years ago, my family and I ate lunch at a restaurant in Boston's Chinatown. My son, Sam, who must have been seven or eight, noticed that we were the only Caucasians in the place: "We're the only ones here who look like Americans." Oh, dear. I'm afraid I corrected him as though I knew better: "Sam, what we look like is Europeans. The other people look like Asians. We all look like Americans." But that was politically correct cant. The truth is that Sam had voiced all too candidly a cultural belief of which virtually no Euro-American is yet completely free.

To think about American culture we have to see past our own biased assumptions about what "looks American," while acknowledging that some traditions remain more influential than others. Groups with power and money dominate the culture and draw others to become like them. Not every history is equal; Americans of every national origin gravitate toward a cultural core defined more by those with power than by those without. America is both a melting pot and a patchwork quilt; each individual and group struggles to achieve a comfortable balance between preserving a distinctive heritage and becoming "American," a process that often tacitly requires adopting norms and values foreign to one's heritage.

Nowhere is this requirement more apparent than in congregations. Catholic churches are more decentralized in polity here than in Europe, because U.S. Catholics come to church with cultural expectations of democracy. Rabbis, who in Europe judged law cases and taught Torah, in America give sermons, offer counseling, raise funds, manage programs, and officiate at weddings, funerals, and b'nai mitzvoth. In short, rabbis in America, for all they do to perpetuate and renew Jewish tradition, behave much like Protestant ministers. Native Americans have lost a great deal of their spiritual inheritance in the course of their oppression by the dominant white culture. Under the extreme stresses of slavery, most African-Americans adopted Christianity; today some are reappropriating African traditions, including Islam, and recasting them in new African-American forms.

And so with respect to money, as in every other sphere, American congregations and their members are subject to divided influence. Sometimes the assumptions of the broader culture pull one way, while family influences, personal temperament, and more particular traditions (including faith traditions) tug in other directions.

Rapid Growth of Income and Consumption

One change that has affected us all in one way or another is rapid economic growth. In two generations, Americans have hit a gradual jackpot: real disposable income per person in the United States has grown to more than three times its 1950 level. Imagine for a moment how boggling it would be to find oneself transported into a world where one's income of, say, $50,000 became $150,000—after inflation. This is the rate of change experienced by the generation that grew up during the Great Depression and fought World War II. Coupled with the movement of jobs from farms to manufacturing and then to services, this rapid economic growth means that virtually all Americans live in a world that is radically new. No indicator of the change is more striking than the upward leap in the amount of money that passes through a family's checkbook. Between 1950 and 2001, spending by households for personal consumption increased, on average, by 2.3 percent after inflation every year. This is almost too small a change to be noticeable, but compounded over 50 years, the average American today consumes 3.2 times more goods and services than our grandparents did.[5] The following chart shows the changes in the average amount of personal income for every American over time. The numbers have been corrected for inflation, so that we can estimate the change in real buying power. The second line shows how much of the average American's income has gone for personal consumption. Both amounts have grown to more than three times their 1950 level. The chart shows the economic slowdowns of the early 1970s, the early 1980s, and the early 1990s, and also shows how little difference these have made in the overall pattern.

Figure 1.1
Real U.S. Income and Consumption per Person[6]

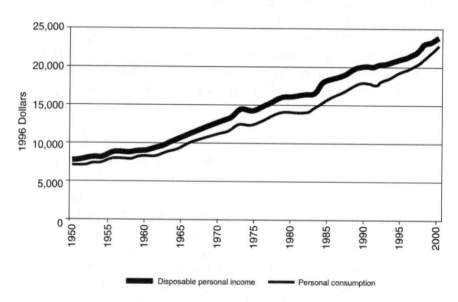

Congregations have benefited from their members' growing wealth, but they must deal also with increased competition for members' time and energy, as people have become able to afford new ways to spend their time. The youth group is no longer the only place for teenagers to go on Sunday evening, and adults have many options—among them travel, boating, rental movies, and Web surfing—to keep them away from worship. Congregations have also experienced growth in their own consumption. Between 1950 and 1997, for example, per-member contributions to the churches in a sample of 11 denominations grew 165 percent after inflation.[7] To be sure, church membership declined somewhat in the same period. Nonetheless, a typical church of 150 members realized 2.6 times as much buying power from its members' gifts in 1997 as 30 years earlier. During most of the period, per-member "benevolence" giving to denominational, missionary, and other causes outside the congregation remained almost flat, so the typical congregation's ability to spend on itself grew even more.[8] If these statistics are representative of religious groups across the spectrum— and I see no reason to doubt it—congregations have participated fully in the rapid increase in consumption that has been a prominent feature of American society since World War II.

Of course, not all of this increased consumption has been a good thing. When there was an extra biscuit on the dinner table, my great-aunt Susie Hotchkiss used to say, "It'll go to waste or it'll go to waist!" To judge from rising rates of obesity, many of us have picked the latter option. Some of our increased household consumption has brought us new or improved products, including television, microwave ovens, medications, computers, and new kinds of telephones. Individually many of the new products seem useful, or at least harmless, though questions about the environmental consequences of so much production and consumption do not cease. The largest increases in consumption have been for services, especially medical, financial, and educational services, and research and development of (guess what!) new products. A big item in the mix is recreation, including large amounts for cable television (which was previously-nonexistent) and casino gambling (which was previously illegal).[9] We may well wonder about the spiritual consequences of these increases, both for those who participate fully and those who lack the resources to do so.

Taken all in all, are our lives better? We're not sure. It is not easy to compare the losses—for example, open space, fresh air, and an easygoing pace of life—against the gains, which include broader access to education, cleaner homes, more varied food, and longer lives. After rapid growth and change, we are uncertain how to judge a world so different from the one in which our parents and grandparents lived.

The Growth of Economic Inequality

Concern about inequality has risen in the past few decades. Up until the mid-1970s, the incomes of rich and poor Americans grew at about the same rate. But between 1977 and 2000, the income of the poorest fifth fell 9 percent while that of the richest fifth grew by 43 percent. By 2000, the top fifth of households was receiving almost half of all personal income, while the poorest fifth received only 3.6 percent.[10] The growing imbalance troubles people who believe that economic inequality tends, over time, to erode political equality, or that the high incomes of elite corporate leaders, entertainers, athletes, and investors are simply not fair.

For the most part, the growth of inequality is the result of the highest personal incomes rising faster than the lowest ones. An additional factor is the concentration of income in two-income households. Doctors once married nurses; now they marry other doctors, while the nurses marry other nurses.

In view of the rapid growth of average personal income, some say that only petty jealousy would lead us to object to the wealth of the wealthy. While acknowledging that people in the poorest group, whose incomes have declined, may need financial assistance, job training, or other help, some argue that the high incomes of the rich are neither the cause nor the result of the low incomes of the poor. Middle and upper-middle incomes have been growing, albeit more slowly than top incomes. What difference does it make, then, that a small group at the top is getting bigger raises than the rest of us?

It may or may not be true that high incomes "cause" low ones, or vice versa, but it is certain that the presence of a rich elite can cause serious practical problems for the poor. In any city, for example, a limited amount of land is available close to the business center. When incomes are relatively equal, developers will create an economic mix of housing—rental apartments, single-family houses, condominiums—within commuting distance. One development might aim for the wealthy with 10-acre lots and mansions and another accommodate blue-collar workers in duplex and triplex houses. The first development will make a profit because of its high prices, the other because of its high density.

But when incomes become so unequal that the wealthiest buyers can pay, if necessary, 50 to 100 times as much per square foot of living space as the poorest can, it no longer makes good business sense to build high-density, affordable housing. Over time, the wealthy bid against each other for the most convenient and attractive space, and prices for the best locations rise. Attracted by high prices, developers convert low-rent apartments into high-priced condominiums, tear down tract houses to build mansions, and design new developments to cater to the rich, who have the money, rather than the poor, who don't. The result, as reported in *Fortune* magazine, is that in the United States, "A record 5.4 million households spend more than half of their income on rent or live in substandard housing."[11]

Barbara Ehrenreich, a New York writer, chronicled the situation of the working poor by temporarily becoming one of them. Working as a waitress, a housecleaner, and a Wal-Mart clerk, she tried to live on what she could earn. The biggest of the many challenges of this experiment, she reports in *Nickel and Dimed*, was finding housing she could afford. On wages of about $1,000 a month—$1,200 when she held two jobs—she had to pay rents of $400 to $625 a month for housing, some of which was squalid and dangerous. Noting that government support of affordable housing has declined, Ehrenreich observes with irony that in real life she receives a $20,000 housing subsidy in the form of tax deductions for homeowners—more than her annual income during the experiment.[12]

The problems of the poor are not new, and by most measures, economic inequality was even higher in the 1920s than it is today. But inequality grew rapidly between the 1970s and 1990, and the resulting changes to our national life are ones we have not yet entirely assimilated.

Most Americans (with a few utopian or socialist exceptions) at least tacitly accept some economic inequality. Without differences of wealth, people would have no incentive to "get ahead," and our society would lose one of its traditional sources of vitality. At the same time we become uncomfortable when inequalities of wealth confront us too directly in our personal lives. In many settings, we tend to associate with people whose income and wealth are similar enough to ours that we can ignore the difference. We become uncomfortable when we learn that inequality can make a difference in our personal relationships. Congregations tend to draw people from a fairly narrow range of economic circumstances. People find homogeneous congregations attractive, and describe them as "comfortable," "friendly," or "accepting." In one church several years ago, during a break in a governing board retreat, I overheard this story:

> Do you remember that guy who came to church in a Cadillac? He wore a suit. I said to myself, "He's not going to fit in here." He parked right out in front in the visitors' parking, and a couple of people made remarks about whether his car would fit. I can tell you, we never saw him again after that day!

This was by no means a poor congregation. In fact, it was predominantly upper-middle class. Out of curiosity I checked the parking lot, and sure enough, there were no Cadillacs—only Volvos, Audis, Saabs, and upper-end Toyotas. Like most congregations, this one had sorted itself out not only by income level but also by automotive taste!

We avoid confronting our unease about economic inequality by distancing ourselves from people who are different, and by trying not to notice the differences. One of the most frequent reasons clergy give for avoiding the financial aspects of congregational life is that they don't want to know how much members give. An Episcopal priest put it to me this way: "If I knew who the biggest givers were, it would make it hard for me to treat everyone equally." What a confession! Is the power of wealth so great that we religious leaders need to cloak ourselves in ignorance to keep free of it? Perhaps so.

Philosopher Jacob Needleman met many wealthy people in the course of writing his book *Money and the Meaning of Life*, and afterward said in an interview:

> First, we have to recognize . . . and not be hypocritical about how much we are influenced by the fact that someone has money. . . . I met someone who has a billion dollars, and suddenly I had a different feeling toward him. I had a different relationship with him. I couldn't help it. Unfortunately, I can't say, "Well, I'm free of that."[13]

Wealth confers an authority upon the wealthy that extends beyond the skill or expertise or luck that gained them wealth. When a few wealthy families give a large share of a congregation's budget, it can be difficult indeed for clergy leaders to treat them just the same as everybody else. Of course, ignorance is not complete protection; what we imagine people give can be as powerful an influence as actual knowledge.

Americans have a special difficulty facing the fact of inequality because egalitarianism is so deep a part of our national philosophy. A minister who has served churches in the United States and England once noted to me that American ministers who move to Britain can be surprised that feudal patterns persist. One young, otherwise radical British member took the new minister aside and informed her that her predecessor had gotten into trouble because he "spoke to Lord X just the way he would speak to anybody else." Many U.S. clergy have found to their chagrin that while few congregations will admit to having such a patron, the reality and the expectation of respectful deference are more widespread than we would like to admit.

It is not only clergy who take a don't-ask-don't-tell approach to differences in wealth. Many commentators have observed that Americans are reluctant to discuss the subject even with their closest friends. Asked how often in the past year they had discussed their incomes with anyone outside their immediate family, 82 percent of the respondents in Princeton sociologist Robert Wuthnow's 1992 survey said they had never or hardly ever done so. Discussing one's giving to charities seems to be even more taboo (or perhaps less interesting as a conversation topic), with 92 percent saying they had never or hardly ever discussed this subject outside the family.[14] This statistic may seem ironic, given the importance of money and wealth-seeking in our value system, but on second thought the importance of money may be what makes it private.

In my experience, most members seriously underestimate the range of wealth and income in the congregation. Whether the question is "How many members of this congregation currently are unemployed?" or "How many millionaires do we have here?" or "How many member families could, if they chose to, give $10,000 or more to a capital campaign?" the estimates are predictably half or less than half of the reality. We are most comfortable when everyone is equal, so we pretend that it is so.

Egalitarianism is a central value of our national culture, and in churches and synagogues one hears concern about social injustice and disparities of wealth. But in the economic realm, we are at most committed to "equal opportunity," not equal wealth—and we do not agree even on what equal opportunity should mean in practice. In many countries the poor resent the wealth of the rich, and class conflict has been the result. Poor and middle-class Americans tend rather to admire the rich and hope one day to be rich themselves. To the proletarians of Europe Karl Marx offered the promise of a scrupulously fair society: "From each according to his abilities, to each according to his needs." But at the same time Marx was writing for Europeans, workers in America were reading tales of plucky young men rising from "rags to riches," written by a former minister, Horatio Alger. Instead of organizing to depose the wealthy, many Americans expect to emulate them. That acute French observer of America, Alexis de Tocqueville, observed as much in 1835. Owing in large part, he thought, to the law of inheritance, which in the United States gives siblings an equal share, "[t]he last trace of hereditary ranks and distinctions is destroyed."

> I do not mean that there is any lack of wealthy individuals in the United States; I know of no country, indeed, where the love of money has taken stronger hold on the affections of men and where a profounder contempt is expressed for the theory of the permanent equality of property. But wealth circulates with inconceivable rapidity, and experience shows that it is rare to find two succeeding generations in the full enjoyment of it.[15]

Most Americans oppose schemes of strict equality partly because we feel that our own opportunities depend on a system that gives us a chance to become wealthy ourselves.

And yet strict egalitarian communities recurrently appear on the fringes of American religious history, most memorably in Oneida, Hopedale, and Brook Farm, where all possessions (theoretically at least) were shared. Such utopian experiments reflect doubts about inequality that still persist. In the back corridors of Christian consciousness are Jesus' warnings about wealth and Paul's exhortations to people of the early church to share their worldly goods among themselves: "The aim is equality; as Scripture has it, 'Those who gathered more did not have too much, and those who gathered less did not have too little.'"[16] While such community sharing is far from the general practice, the thought persists that at least within the congregation, inequalities of wealth are a bit scandalous, and best downplayed or ignored. One clear symptom of this feeling is the resistance that meets efforts to give special recognition to the largest givers. Despite much evidence that such recognition is effective in encouraging large gifts, many churches pride themselves on a policy of strict equality in recognizing all gifts, even, in some cases, gifts of nothing.

Synagogues have generally been more comfortable with inequality of wealth—or at least more willing to recognize large givers by encouraging them to announce their gifts, and by affixing plaques and naming buildings for them. Until recently, only a few synagogues eschewed such recognitions on principle. An increasing number of congregations now have begun to question traditional ways of funding the congregation, and among other reforms have declared themselves "plaque-free." (One such synagogue with which I recently consulted declared its unofficial trademark to be the toothbrush!) Discomfort about inequality of wealth is a part of American culture that touches every faith community.

Overwork and Underwork

One reason economic inequality has grown is that some households have too much paid work and others have too little. In recent decades, unemployment has been relatively low, and people with jobs have been working greatly increased hours. These rosy statistics obscure the increase in the number of Americans underemployed—working, but at jobs that do not use their full capacities, or that pay less than they need to live on.

In the decade or two after World War II, the average number of paid work hours per American declined. This trend surprised no one; productivity—the amount of goods and services a worker can produce in an hour's time—increased 127 percent between 1947 and 1972, mostly because of new technology. Since then, productivity has grown a bit more slowly; by 2000, it was up again, this time by 62 percent, to two and two-thirds times its 1947 level.[17] The science-fiction futures of the 1950s and '60s routinely assumed that the workweek would decline as productivity increased, until sooner or later humans would do nothing but wait for our robots to bring us our drinks. It didn't happen.

When people can create more value with the same amount of work (that is, when productivity grows), society as a whole has a choice: it can keep its consumption the same and reduce the amount of time spent working, or it can keep work hours the same and increase consumption. Since 1970 or so, American society has chosen both to work more and to consume more. In a landmark study published as *The Overworked American* in

1992, economist Juliet Schor estimated that Americans with full-time jobs worked 1,786 hours in 1969 and 1,949 hours in 1987, an increase of 167 hours, or almost an extra month every year. The added hours came in the form of increased moonlighting and overtime, reduced vacations, and increases in the normal hours expected, especially of salaried employees.[18] In 1992 Robert Wuthnow found that

> [d]espite the fact that 66 percent of the labor force said they are working harder than they were five years ago (and 52 percent would like to work fewer hours), 68 percent say they would be willing to work even longer hours each week to earn more money. Nearly half say they would do less interesting work or take a higher pressure job if, in either case, they could make more money. And these figures are as high among people who are already in the upper third of the income scale as among those with lower incomes.[19]

Wuthnow's data differ from a survey done in 1978 by the U.S. Department of Labor, which asked workers whether they would sacrifice part of a raise in pay in favor of more time off. Eighty-four percent said they would take the time off and sacrifice at least some money.[20] It seems clear to me that in many households, people who protest that they would gladly sacrifice some income to have more time for their family do not do it when they have the chance. The lure of an ever-growing selection of consumer goods, and in some cases the intrinsic satisfactions of the work itself, explains why people choose to work long hours, or perhaps more accurately, why they fail to resist pressure from employers and peers to fall in with the trend toward work.

In the larger view, it may not matter much what workers prefer, because they may not have a choice. At lower income levels, moonlighting is a practical necessity, largely to pay inflated housing expenses. Employers typically offer even higher-earning workers a take-it-or-leave it choice—long hours or no job.

Like the concentration of wealth, the growing workweek has been compounded by a sharp increase in the number of women employed outside the home. Consequently, that the number of hours worked per person has increased even more than the number of hours per worker. The result is familiar to all clergy: life's center of gravity in many families has shifted from home and neighborhood to workplace, school, mall, soccer field, and fast-food restaurant. Congregations dominated by retirees often find younger adults puzzling, because so many of them construe congregational life in vocational terms. Younger adults will volunteer, but only if the volunteer experience is carefully planned, efficient, and short-term. They often lack the social graces and tolerance for imperfection that once made congregational life workable, and in their place bring "skillsets" and standards of "quality" from the workplace.

The Separation of Money from Faith

It is not surprising, given the rapid rate of change in economic life, that we experience a disjunction between the choices we must make about money and the teachings of our faith traditions. The disjunction is not new; it has deep roots in religious warnings against greed and other economic sins. The Jewish teacher Maimonides, for instance, stressed that one should "eat, drink, and provide for one's household according to one's income and not become overly involved in business as a result of increased expenses."[21]

The New Testament contains a variety of statements about wealth. At one moment Jesus seems to say that the only way to heaven is to give away all one's possessions,[22] and at another, that we should be prudent stewards of God's gifts.[23] These statements are not easy to reconcile, perhaps because they stem not from Jesus' attitudes toward wealth per se, but from his worry that wealth might draw people's attention away from more important values. Biblical scholar Sondra Ely Wheeler summarized her study of New Testament texts about possessions this way:

> The dangers of distraction and entanglement, of misplaced trust and loyalty that inhere in ownership are all brought forward, but there is no repudiation of material goods as such. . . . the same epistles that condemn greed as idolatrous can command provision for oneself and one's family as a duty. . . .
>
> Material wealth is problematic because it is often a hindrance to heeding the gospel; it is dangerous because it is a temptation to the sin of idolatry; it is suspect because it is frequently the result or the means of social injustice; finally its disposition is a matter of great moral weight, as the response to human needs is a sign of

the advent of God's kingdom and a test of the love that identifies
Jesus' true followers.[24]

In this analysis, the goal of the New Testament writers was not so much to
specify how people's economic lives should change as it was to place money
in its right relation to the larger loyalties for which Jesus had lived and died.

In many if not most American congregations, religion no longer offers
an effective counterweight to the pressures of the broader culture, at least
where money is concerned. The teachings of religion seem too unrealistic,
too otherworldly, to serve as practical guides to economic action. This trend
is partly a consequence of the rapid rate of economic change, not only in
the past half-century, but also since the beginning of the Industrial Revolution
in the 18th century.

Wuthnow suggests that "America underwent industrialization never
feeling fully at ease with its social, cultural, and moral consequences."[25]
How could anyone imagine, much less discuss and form consensus, on the
enormous changes that have come in the past 200 years? Would any
reasonable community have voted to adopt steam-powered manufacturing,
knowing in advance how much air pollution the burning of that much coal
would cause? Would the public, in 1900, have chosen to allow automobiles
to be invented and deployed if they had known that, by 1999, we would
accept, more or less without complaint, some 40,000 dead and 3 million
injured every year in traffic accidents?[26] Probably not, but more to the
point, it is never possible to ask such questions in advance. Instead we
struggle afterward, using values shaped in an earlier time, to reconcile the
changes that have come about. It is not surprising, after so much rapid
change, that we have difficulty drawing clear connections between the
economic and religious portions of our lives.

Ancient traditions provide problematic guidance, because when texts
speak of money, they address times when money functioned differently.
For example, the Book of Exodus, the Qur'an, and the early councils of the
Christian church all condemn "usury," or money lending at interest.[27] This
prohibition reflects the attitude of societies in which lending was usually a
way to exploit the poor. As trade and industry took hold in Europe and
around the world, businesspeople had to raise money to invest in goods,
factories, and machines. Sufficient capital could be available to firms
only if investors could count on compensation for the use of their money.
Medieval Christians dealt with the problem by relegating money lending
to the Jews (who adapted their own understanding of the Bible to allow

them to oblige), but finally the Christian concept of usury was softened to ban only interest that was excessive.[28] Islamic law still theoretically prohibits loans at interest altogether, but Muslims have created various circumventions of this rule to accommodate the needs of a global economy that could not operate without credit.

Religious traditions about money arose in settings so different from the present that many of them have had to be severely tailored and adjusted. Consequently many people compartmentalize, assuming that faith has little to say about the economic world and, by default, live without economic guidance from religion. When we relegate money to a realm apart from the sources of our most enduring values, we should not be surprised that our feelings about money become confused.

One way people express the separation of money and faith is by calling them both "private." Just as it is not polite to question my religious beliefs, it is rude to raise questions about my financial choices. Faith and money are so private in our culture that we can avoid serious conversation about either one, and certainly a conversation that brings one to bear upon the other. Clergy who attempt to start such a conversation violate a powerful taboo— a taboo that exists in part to protect us from the anxiety our mixed feelings would arouse if we examined them more closely. To many clergy it feels risky to encourage congregants to criticize their own assumptions about money from the standpoint of faith. Faithful ministry under these conditions is not easy. But it is essential, because the money choices people face each day are not, at bottom, technical questions that can be solved by a financial analyst. Money represents time and energy. It confers power and status. It is the medium through which we carry out some of our most important responsibilities and extend some of our most practical help to others. If religion is to mean anything, it has to influence the way we manage money choices.

But American culture divides economics from religion. It places money in a sphere governed by power, calculation, market forces, and self-interest, even to the point of selfishness and callous disregard for human suffering. Some people accept this state of affairs as a necessary evil; others claim that ultimately (or, as economists would say, "in the long run") it serves the public good. For people who work in the economic sphere, it can be difficult indeed to connect the guiding principles of economics to religion, which in recent decades has spoken mostly in the language of compassion, family life, and personal relationships.

Soft, compassionate "religious" values stand in contrast to hard-hearted, "businesslike" decision making. I will exaggerate a bit to make this distinction clear: Religion, in this way of thinking, ought to stay in the domestic sphere where kindness, generosity, and mercy rule, while business, personal finance, and economic policy should, while perhaps aiming at the same ultimate goals, be guided day to day by harsher values. These compartments roughly correspond to the traditional spheres of men and women, marketplace and home. Clergy occupy a midpoint in this cosmology, leading congregations populated mainly by women, whose discourse is confined to the home vocabulary, and who are regarded as incompetent to speak truth to the economic powers still held by wealthy men (or these days, sometimes wealthy women playing roles defined by men). This mind-set reinforces the taboo on conversation about money in congregations and confines clergy to an awkward mediating role: espousing the "soft" values of the home, while accommodating (and, as institutional leaders, perforce sometimes living by) the "hard" values of the marketplace.

Another aspect of the division between economic and religious life is the attitude toward consumption or materialism that is normative in each realm. Economists measure our "standard of living" by the amount we can consume, as reflected by the gross domestic product (GDP), gross personal expenditures (GPE), and similar measures. We sometimes say "the quality of life" when we mean the quantity of goods and services we can consume. The bumper sticker "He who dies with the most toys wins" states a philosophy few would espouse but most would recognize. Materialism, the belief that possessions, consumption, and wealth are central sources of life's meaning—or on a more practical level, the habit of organizing one's life around money and consumption—is an important and persistent trait of our national character.

If hyperconsumption is the norm that rules the economic sphere, a different standard is applied to congregations. Concern about the wealth and privileges of the clergy fueled a good part of the Reformation, especially in its more radical expressions, so it is no surprise that in the United States, where many of the formative roots are Protestant, suspicion of the clergy's motives has been a recurrent theme. With notable exceptions (for example, Hicksite Quakers), Americans accept the need for a paid clergy, but concern about churches' and synagogues' materialism is widespread. In Wuthnow's 1992 survey, 36 percent of the total labor force and 24 percent of weekly churchgoers said, "It annoys me when churches ask me to give money."

Similar percentages did not agree that "Churches use the money they get wisely and responsibly."[29] Clearly, a substantial minority of the U.S. public views congregations with some distrust, and the perception that congregations and clergy act out of self-interest seems to play a major part in this attitude.

The charge that religious institutions are a covert scheme to bilk the innocent has dogged the clergy throughout American history. The accusation draws some of its force from the fact that it has sometimes been justified. The fictional evangelist Elmer Gantry in Sinclair Lewis's novel represents rapacious clergy behavior that millions of Americans have experienced, or believe they have. From ancient times to our own, there is no lack of evidence for those who wish to view the clergy in this way. But in most cases, distrust of religious institutions stems not from serious abuses but from the application of a standard of behavior out of sync with the rest of society. Because people of all ages are subjected to a continual barrage of propaganda aimed at influencing their use of money, congregations, if they are to have a chance, need to find a way to ask for money that is more effective—and maybe also less annoying.

There's nothing wrong with congregations' advocating values different from those of the marketplace. Offering such challenges to culture is among the central functions of religion. But when religion and decisions about money are sealed off from interchange, the culture is deprived of the redemptive possibilities of faith, and religious institutions are pushed to the margin and made ineffective. The boundary between the religious and the economic can block congregations from extending powerful kinds of pastoral care to those affected by job loss, discrimination, and poor stewardship of household resources. It can also block congregations' social witness, limit the scope of their ethical influence, and keep them poor.

Pushed to the edge of the economy, religious bodies find it harder to attract talented candidates for ordination. Once settled, a low-paid clergyperson is apt to move on for reasons unrelated to the rhythms of the congregation's life; for instance, when the spouse accepts a job in a more highly compensated field. Perhaps most seriously, isolation from the economic side of life leads clergy to favor timid, careful kinds of leadership over bold or disruptive kinds. All these effects tend to diminish the clergy leader's influence and status—even if all concerned sincerely think they do not care much about money.

Taken together, our culture's teachings hamstring clergy, keeping them from giving effective leadership where money is concerned. There are exceptions—for example, those African-American churches that allow clergy to give bolder leadership in matters of money. A few congregations have organized conversations about workplace ethics, personal finance, and charitable giving, or programs of debt counseling, community investment, and cooperative housing. These experiments stretch cords of tentative communication across a boundary that has been closed too long.

CHAPTER 2

A Quick Sketch
of Your Personal Finances

If those who gain all they can, save all they can, will likewise give all they can, then the more they gain, the more they grow in grace, and the more treasure they lay up in heaven.

John Wesley

To give self-confident leadership on money issues, it is important that clergy grow in awareness of our own attitudes, aptitudes, and anxieties, and get a grip on our own household finances. Unfortunately the financial lives of many clergy are in disarray. This state of affairs is due partly, but by no means only, to our being underpaid. A low salary does not always lead to financial disorder. Many people who have problems making ends meet on a family income of $25,000 have the same problems when their incomes rise to $50,000 or $100,000. But other people manage to adjust their spending as their income changes, keeping a steady rate of savings even in lean times.

Overspending is not the only kind of money problem, though in our consumer-oriented, easy-credit economy it is one of the most common. Some people obsess about their money, spending too much time accounting for it and investing it, so that it interferes with more enjoyable and productive ways of spending time. Others, whose budgets are in balance, feel driven to advance to ever higher levels of compensation. These people work harder and cling to jobs longer than is healthy for them and their families. And some people find financial stability boring, and need always to be engaged in some risky gamble.

You don't have to be rich to give effective money leadership. You do need to have a firm grip on whatever money troubles are distracting you, and to be clear about the personal anxieties and insecurities that hamper you. If anxiety about your personal finances undermines your leadership, take steps to get an accurate bird's-eye view of your financial situation, to identify what actions are needed to get your finances in hand, and to begin making basic choices about the theology and values that will guide you in the future. Once you have taken even a step or two toward fiscal stability and solvency, you will grow in your authority to guide and encourage others.

Beginning the Sketch

Most people do not have an accurate mental picture of their own financial situation. It is easy to put off looking at your money situation, fearing what you might discover. Or you may simply not know where to start.

This chapter provides a simple method for evaluating your personal finances. Sacrificing precision for efficiency, we'll sketch a rough outline of your money that will fit on the back of an envelope (well, maybe a big envelope). At the end of the chapter is a list of resources to help you go further and learn more about personal finances. In the meantime, we'll draw a picture that is truthful, if not necessarily precise to the penny.

Two brief comments before we start: If you have a spouse or partner, how you follow these directions will depend on how the two of you handle your money. If you are one of those couples who keep money (and perhaps other things as well) completely separate, it probably makes sense to do this exercise on your own. Other couples manage all their money jointly; if that's you, then follow the instructions as though the two of you were one person. If you're in between, you'll have to make a judgment about what to do.

In any case, you may want to mention to your spouse that you are doing this exercise. Money is a leading marital *casus belli*, and it is not wise couple politics to become too enthusiastic about financial reform before inviting your partner to jump onto the bandwagon with you.

My second comment: If you are already using Quicken, Microsoft Money, or another computer home-finance program, you may have handy much of the information I will ask for. Or you may not. These programs succeed in the marketplace partly by allowing people to manage their finances without keeping track of every penny. The trouble is, they also allow you not to watch every dollar, or every thousand dollars. If you take advantage of this "feature," you can end up with neatly printed statements that are so far off as to be useless. So as you follow the instructions as I give them, use primary documents like bank and brokerage statements to verify your printouts.

The Ghost of Money Past

The first step is to calculate a number you may find astounding: your total lifetime earnings. Visit the Social Security Administration Web site at *www.ssa.gov*, and request a copy of your social security statement. (You can also ask for it by phone from your local social security office.) The SSS contains a list of the earnings on which you paid social security tax each year, and an estimate of the benefit you will be likely to receive if you retire or are disabled.

When you receive the SSS, check to make sure all income is listed that should be. Salaries, wages, honoraria, and other employment income reported on your tax return should be included. In general, the number for each year should equal the income you reported on Schedule SE of your federal income tax return. If you find a discrepancy, the statement has instructions for correcting it.

Some kinds of income do not appear on the SSS. Clergy who object to receiving social security benefits can exempt themselves. Until the Internal Revenue Service cracked down in the 1980s, a good many clergy helped themselves to an exemption not because they objected to the benefits, but because they objected to the tax. If you have ever been exempt, you'll have to dig through your old tax returns to add up your income. If you had income that you did not report on your return at all—whether legally or not—it will of course not show on the SSS either. Think unreported tips, baby-sitting, and other teenage jobs. Think wedding cash that somehow melded with the money in your pocketbook without your writing it down, net winnings from your weekly poker game (you wish!), and any money you received from drug deals, bank heists, or those $20 bills you print up in the basement. Unless you reported income from these things on Form 1040, you will need to add them to the list by hand.

If you have received large gifts of cash or property, inheritances, life-insurance benefits, divorce settlements, child-support or alimony payments, they did not count as earned income; but for our purposes they should be listed. We want an honest total of all money that has flowed into your life.

At this point we are leaving investment income out—money produced by money. Bank interest, stock dividends, and capital gains are taxed as income, but not as earnings, so they don't show up on the SSS. That's OK; at this point we are not interested in investment income.

Once you have listed everything you can remember, add up the figures and be amazed. If you are 40 or 50 years old and have worked steadily since you graduated from college, you very likely have received between $500,000 and $1 million in your lifetime. Even people who have had long breaks in employment often find this exercise surprising. Joe Dominguez, an influential lecturer and writer on personal finance, told the story of a woman who had been a homemaker most of her life. When she divorced, she felt guilty about accepting her share of the marital assets, because, in her mind, she had made no financial contribution to the marriage. And she felt unprepared to re-enter the paid workforce. She sent away for her social security statement, added it up, and learned that she had earned over $15,000 from odd jobs during those years of her marriage when she was contributing "nothing." In the mirror of that statement she saw herself for the first time as a competent wage earner. Merely taking this step gave her the confidence to apply for and land a job at twice the salary she had previously assumed she was worth.[1]

Adding up your lifetime earnings probably won't change your image of yourself quite that much, but it might!

The Ghost of Money Present

The second step toward getting a handle on your finances is to look at what you own and what you owe. The difference between these numbers is your "net worth," the amount you would have if you sold everything, paid your debts, and started fresh. You know how much money you've received in your lifetime. Your net worth tells how much you have left. If you got hit by a falling steeple, your net worth would be what your heirs would have to fight over (minus probate costs and taxes, and plus life insurance).To figure your net worth, you make a balance sheet.

What You Own (Assets)

First, list the things you own, your assets. If you leave off the pennies, the arithmetic will be much simpler. In fact, you can round any item over a thousand to the nearest hundred and still get a reasonably precise result.

Cash and securities. Start with the cash in your pocket. Write it down. Find the current balance in each of your bank accounts. If you don't reconcile your bank accounts each month, find your last statement and use the "closing balance" number. Add savings bonds and certificates of deposit, including those you have forgotten. (Incidentally, forgetting about certificates of deposit and U.S. Savings Bonds can be a wonderful investment strategy!) For CDs the bank can tell you the current value, including interest. For savings bonds, a Web site at *www.treasurydirect.gov* will help you calculate the current value.

Mutual funds send statements every month listing the value of your holdings. If you own securities like stocks or corporate bonds, the stockbroker who holds them for you probably sends a monthly or quarterly statement with their current value. That statement may show a cash balance, too; add that to the list. If you own securities but don't get a statement, ask for one.

Other financial assets. With any luck at all, you don't own cash-value (also known as "whole," "ordinary," or "straight") life insurance. Unless you are quite wealthy, such policies are almost always poor investments. If you do own one, list its cash value as an asset and look into replacing it with term insurance.

You may own stock options, REITs (real-estate investment trusts), limited oil-drilling partnerships, or any of a thousand other instruments of torture out of Wall Street. If so, I'm truly sorry. Call the stockbroker or brother-in-law who got you into them and ask what they're worth, if anything. While you're at it, ask what it would cost you to get out of them. (If you know what you're doing and are willing to spend lots of time tracking, trading, and adjusting these investments, then I suggest that you should get a life!)

Durable consumer goods. Walk around your house, noting any large and expensive items. Your large-screen television qualifies. So do your kids' computer, the exercise machine under the cobwebs in the basement, and any major furniture you wouldn't be embarrassed to give to your congregation's rummage sale. Write down an estimated resale value for each one. If you bought it new and it still works and looks like new, write down half of what you paid for it. Otherwise write less. With this method, you'll overestimate the value of the big stuff, which makes up for all the little stuff we are ignoring. This is not science; it's for the back of an envelope.

Do not include things that belong to your landlord or that you would sell with your house; for example, the refrigerator, washer, dryer, or pool filter. If you own them and would take them with you when you move, count them.

Your car or cars are probably the one item for which ascertaining an accurate value is worthwhile. You can find the "blue book" value of your car on several Web sites, including the official *Kelley Blue Book* site at *www.kbb.com*. Use the figure for the "trade-in" price, which is an estimate of what you would get if you sold the car to a dealer. Be brutally honest when you are asked at the Web site about the car's condition.

Retirement plans. These days most denominational and employer-sponsored retirement plans (the ones called "defined-contribution plans") send a quarterly statement that shows your balance in dollars, even though the money may be invested in 10 countries. Old-fashioned pension plans ("defined-benefit plans") don't show you a dollar balance because you don't have one. Instead the sponsor promises to pay you a pension calculated according to the plan's rules. The plan administrator can give you the "present value" of this kind of account. Add it in.

IRAs, 403(b) and 401(k) plans, tax-sheltered college-savings plans, and other such long-term savings should go on the list, too. You should have a statement dated sometime in the last three months; if not, call the bank or brokerage that holds the account and ask for your balance.

Real estate. If you own land, a house, or other real estate, you need to estimate what you could sell it for. For many people, these assets have by far the largest dollar value, and are the hardest to pin down accurately. Luckily, for this purpose we don't need to do it accurately; probably it's better to do it conservatively. Most real-estate agents are happy to provide a rough, off-the-record appraisal of your house in the hope that you'll be so pleased you'll let them sell it for you.

What You Owe (Liabilities)

Now we'll take a look at the downside: what you owe, your liabilities. Start a new list, and put the following items on it:

Credit cards. I know, I know, this is the painful part for some of you. But trust me, if credit card debt is a problem for you, adding up the total is the beginning of relief. If we were doing this properly, we'd pick a date and determine your exact debt level at a given time. For this purpose, just find the most recent bill for each card (if you didn't file your bills, don't worry; you'll get new ones) and find the total amount owed (not the minimum payment, sometimes reassuringly called the "amount due." You'll recognize the total amount owed by the fact that it is probably the largest number on the page. If you've made a payment since the bill came (but before you counted your cash for the assets list), you can subtract what you paid from the amount.

By the way, cards from Sears or Macy's or Home Depot are credit cards. If you carry an outstanding balance, list it.

Auto loans. Same drill: find the latest statement; put your unpaid balance on the list. Or call the bank and ask. If you have paid since the statement but before you counted your bank balances, subtract the payment.

Academic loans. Too many of us owe too much to dear old alma mater (or the U.S. government's student loan programs). Get the current balance and put it down.

Credit lines. You may have a line of credit at your bank, which is basically a card-free credit card. If you've used it and not paid it off, your bank statement will show your outstanding balance, which should go on the balance sheet as a liability.

Quarterly tax payments. Many clergy pay income and self-employment taxes quarterly. The advantage is that we get to keep the money till it's due, and the disadvantage is that it may have burned a hole in our pockets by that time. If you have a tax payment due soon, you owe a debt to Uncle Sam. List it as a liability.

Home mortgage. You may or may not get a statement from your bank or mortgage company that gives your outstanding balance. If not, call your mortgage lender and ask. If you have a home equity loan in addition to your main mortgage, that's a liability also.

What's Left (Net Worth)

This one is easy. Subtract your liabilities from your assets. The difference is your net worth, sometimes called equity or net assets. Here's an example of a finished balance sheet:

Table 2.1

Rev. Dr. Elizabeth Grable			
Balance Sheet			
November 2001			
ASSETS	**Interest rate**		
Cash in purse		$	28
Checking acount			368
Money market fund			2,600
CD at Jimmy's Bank			1,100
Home theater			400
1999 Toyota Corolla			8,600
Ministers' retirement fund			62,400
House: 39 Rodeo Drive			247,000
TOTAL ASSETS		$	**322,496**
LIABILITIES			
MasterCard	19%	$	1,300
Nordstrom's card	15.5%		252
Checking line of credit	21%		4,200
Seminary loans	6.75%		18,200
Taxes due Jan. 15, 2002	0%		840
Loan on Corolla	7%		8,000
Morgage on 39 Rodeo Dr.	8%		192,300
TOTAL LIABILITIES		$	**225,092**
		$	**97,404**
NET WORTH			

The Rev. Dr. Grable (Betty to her friends) found her net worth of $97,404 an encouraging surprise. You, too, may find that your net worth is larger than you would have expected from the difficulty you have getting by from week to week. That is because the balance sheet, useful as it is, provides only a bird's-eye view of your financial status. To get a more mundane grip on the subject, I suggest an adjusted balance sheet called a "working capital report." To create it, start with the balance sheet you just constructed and eliminate some items. Drop the TV set, the computer, the car, and other stuff that you could sell only at an extreme loss. Eliminate your house and any other real estate, and your retirement plans. Keep only cash and assets you could easily convert to cash, like bank accounts, CDs, and money someone owes you that you're confident will be repaid within a year.

On the liability side, keep credit cards and credit lines. Drop any long-term loans, those that are set up to be paid over several years—your mortgage, and probably your home equity line, though you should keep the equity line if you use it as a credit card. Drop any seminary loans and any other liabilities that will take more than a year to pay. (If we were going to be really scientific about this, we would take all of those long-term loans and keep the amount due in the next 12 months. But we're not.)

Table 2.2

Rev. Dr. Elizabeth Grable				
Working Capital Report				
November 2001				
CURRENT ASSETS	**Interest rate**			
Cash in purse			$	28
Checking acount				368
Money market fund				2,600
CD at Jimmy's Bank				1,100
TOTAL CURRENT ASSETS			$	**4,096**
CURRENT LIABILITIES				
MasterCard	19%		$	1,300
Nordstrom's card	15.5%			252
Checking line of credit	21%			4,200
Taxes due Jan. 15, 2002				840
TOTAL CURRENT LIABILITIES			$	**6,592**
NET WORTH			$	**(2,496)**

As in the sad case of the Rev. Dr. Betty, most clergy find "net working capital" on the expurgated statement less impressive than net worth on the balance sheet. Net worth tells you what your heirs would have if you died—nice for your heirs, but not of much use to you. Net working capital is what you'd have to live on if you lost your job. Poor Betty would have less than nothing. Her net working capital is negative $2,496 (that's why it's in parentheses on the chart). A good short-term financial goal for her would be to increase net working capital until it reaches zero and then keep going until it equals from three to six months' salary.

OK. Now we have a history of all the money that has come into your life since you became a working adult, and two snapshots of what you have to show for it today. The first snapshot (net worth) measures how much you have altogether, and the second (net working capital) measures how much you have available for daily use. We now have most of the facts we need for a reality check on your lifelong relationship with money.

Prophecies of Money Future

Compare your total lifetime earnings with your current net worth. How much of what you've earned do you still have? Theoretically, it's possible to own more than you earned. If that's true for you, congratulations on your thrift and on your luck in the housing and stock markets. Apparently you saved and invested a high fraction of your income, and your investments have earned enough to pay for everything you've spent over the years.

For many people, though, lifetime earnings are astonishingly high and net worth discouragingly low. Your net worth may even be negative: 18 percent of U.S. households had a negative net worth in 1998.[2] It is amazing how much money flows through our hands and how little of it sticks. If this is the case for you, and you want to retire in comfort, you need to learn to spend significantly less than you earn.

How does it happen? To get a clue, our next step is to create a back-of-the-envelope estimate of your income and expenses for the past year. If you keep track of your income and expenses, you may think, "That's easy—I've already done this." But in reality, very few people succeed at keeping track of every penny they earn and spend. Even fewer verify that their income and expense records jibe with the rise and fall of their bank balances. For the back of our envelope, we're going to start with the bank and loan balances, and infer how much you've spent from how much they've changed.

If you keep books on a convenient single-entry system like Quicken or Microsoft Money, brace yourself for a surprise. You may find that your books are less accurate than you thought.

First, you need to make another balance sheet. (I should have warned you about this, but I didn't want to scare you off.) Take your balance sheet and add a second column. For each of the amounts you put into your balance sheet, put into the second column the amount for a date one year before the date you used for the first column. Some of the amounts you'll have to guess; for instance, you might just assume you had the same amount of pocket money then as now.

Here's what Betty got:

Table 2.3

Rev. Dr. Elizabeth Grable			
Balance Sheet			
November 2000-01			
ASSETS	**Interest rate**	**2001**	**2000**
Cash in purse		$ 28	50
Checking acount		368	1,300
Money market fund		2,600	2,200
CD at Jimmy's Bank		1,100	1,050
Home theater		400	400
1999 Toyota Corolla		8,600	9,000
Ministers' retirement fund		62,400	68,000
House: 39 Rodeo Drive		247,000	245,000
TOTAL ASSETS		**$ 322,496**	**327,000**
LIABILITIES			
MasterCard	19%	$ 1,300	4,200
Nordstrom's card	15.5%	252	0
Checking line of credit	21%	4,200	5,300
Seminary loans	6.75%	18,200	18,800
Taxes due Jan. 15	0%	840	840
Loan on Corolla	7%	8,000	3,200
Morgage on 39 Rodeo Dr.	8%	192,300	193,100
TOTAL LIABILITIES		**$ 225,092**	**225,440**
NET WORTH		**$ 97,404**	**101,560**
CHANGE IN NET WORTH		**$ (4,156)**	

Notice that her net worth declined during the year by \$4,156. That's not good. It means that she spent \$4,156 more than she received in income.

Why did we figure it this way, instead of estimating spending and income directly? It can be useful to keep track of your spending and earning directly by setting up a budget, recording each transaction, and so on. But that process involves hundreds of transactions, and is prone to error and self-deception. Professional bookkeepers track almost every penny, and so do some ordinary people (OK, I admit it: I do myself). But at the end of the month, the pros test their records by performing a "trial balance." Essentially they compare income with expense and starting net worth with ending net worth. In theory, the differences should match. In practice, 99 percent of the time there's a discrepancy, and 77 percent of the time the error is in income and expense, because net worth is much easier to figure.[3] For this rough sketch, we're skipping the income and expense step and going with the easier and more reliable net worth comparison.

Actually we're making it even easier than that, because we're going to compare working capital instead of net worth. That way we don't have to worry about gains and losses on investments, depreciation on your car, and other arcane kinds of income and expense. We're going to worry only about cash in and cash out, which is the way most people naturally think about their budget anyway.

Having added a second column to the balance sheet, Betty found it a snap to add a second column to her working-capital report. The \$4,156 decline in her net worth had her a bit depressed. But the working capital comparison gave a more hopeful picture:

Table 2.4

Rev. Dr. Elizabeth Grable
Working Capital Report
November 2000-01

CURRENT ASSETS	Interest rate	2001	2000
Cash in purse		$ 28	50
Checking acount		368	1,300
Money market fund		2,600	2,200
CD at Jimmy's Bank		1,100	1,050
TOTAL CURRENT ASSETS		**$ 4,096**	**4,600**
CURRENT LIABILITIES			
MasterCard	19%	$ 1,300	4,200
Nordstrom's card	15.5%	252	0
Checking line of credit	21%	4,200	5,300
Taxes due Jan. 15	0%	840	840
TOTAL CURRENT LIABILITIES		**$ 6,592**	**10,340**
NET WORKING CAPITAL		**$ (2,496)**	**(5,740)**
CHANGE IN NET WORKING CAPITAL		**$ 3,244**	

While Betty's net worth went down, her working capital went up. It went from minus $5,740 to minus $2,496, an improvement of $3,244. (Going from a big negative number to a small one is going "up.") How can net worth go south while working capital goes north? The main reason is that the stock market declined, taking Betty's denominational retirement fund— and her net worth—with it. That can be unnerving, and it would be important if Betty were about to retire. But since she is more than 10 years from retirement, she can expect to see many market ups and downs over the years. With any luck at all, the ups will more than balance out the downs. For right now, the improvement in Betty's working capital is more important, because it indicates that she is spending less than she earns. She is using what's left over to pay down debt and build up savings.

Betty saved $3,244 out of her income this year. Her income (including salary and housing allowance) is $50,000, so her "savings rate" is just over 6.5 percent. It may seem odd to say so, given that at the end of the year she had no "savings." But she had less debt, which is just as good—the interest she won't pay next year is money she can spend or save, and unlike savings account interest, she won't have to pay taxes on it!

One kind of savings not reflected in the working capital comparison is the $6,000 contribution Betty's church made to her retirement fund. We can legitimately count that, too, as money saved (and money earned), which raises Betty's total savings to $9,244, her income to $56,000, and her resulting savings rate to 16.5 percent. Other adjustments she could make include payments on the principal (not interest!) of her home mortgage or seminary loans. If she chose to make a major lump-sum payment on one of these loans, I'd count it (though Betty would have been smarter to pay down her credit cards first). But I'd pay the most attention to the unadjusted working capital comparison, because that is the clearest measure of how well Betty is managing the resources under her day-to-day control.

Is Betty's 6.5 percent savings rate good? Is her adjusted rate of 16.5 percent enough? There is no simple answer; it depends on what she's saving for. You can go only so far in finances on facts alone. Once you've collected basic facts, the right way to manage your finances depends on the results you want. The next chapter will explore values more deeply, but first here are some "if-then" statements to consider as you look at the sketch you've drawn of your life in money.

Truth and Consequences

Numbers can't tell you how much you should spend, save, or borrow. What numbers can tell you is what will happen if you make certain choices. Using your personal finance snapshot, consider these "if-then" statements:

Outspending Your Earnings

If your working capital declined, you're spending more than you earned. You can stem an outward flow of working capital in only two ways: earning more or spending less. Deciding which to do involves making moral choices: time versus money, spending versus saving, sometimes even money versus integrity. Whether to correct the situation is not a moral choice at all, because in the long run, if you don't correct the situation, it will correct itself. You can only go so far into debt before no one will lend you any more money, and then you have to cut expenses, even if that means becoming a bag gentleman or lady. It is better to take care of it voluntarily.

For many clergy, the surest way to earn more money would be to get into a new profession or return to an old one. Barring those options, it is worth considering whether you should ask for more money in your current situation or apply for a new one. If you have a spouse, he or she could possibly make changes to increase the family income. These are not easy questions, but if it is necessary, one can almost always find some way to increase income.

Most people find, though, that however successful they are at making more money, they generally manage to spend it. Sooner or later, every family needs to figure out how to limit spending. As you look at your side-by-side working capital statements, if you wonder where the money went, you have a lot of company.

You can probably say about how much you make in a year; it is more difficult to guess how much you spend. Some people manage to count every penny, but most of us fail at this pretty miserably. Luckily there is another way, based on the fact that your income and expenses cause changes in your working capital. If you calculate your working capital for the beginning and the end of a year (as we have already done) and add up your cash income, including salary and housing allowance, honoraria, child support, and so on, you can figure out how much you spent during the year. Your working capital at the beginning of the year, plus your income, minus your expenses, equals your working capital at the end. You can use this fact to estimate how much you've spent. Here is the formula:

> \+ starting working capital
> \+ income
> \- ending working capital
> = the amount you spent

For example, if you started out with $20,000, earned $50,000, and ended up with $30,000, you must have spent $40,000—good for you for living within your means! In Betty's case the computation is a little trickier because some of the numbers are negative. She started out with minus $5,740 and earned $50,000; the sum of those is $44,240. Subtracting her ending balance of $2,496 (which is the same as adding $2,496) gives $46,756, the amount she must have spent during the year.

What did she spend it on? Up to now we have avoided keeping track of day-to-day expenses, and we can put that off again by simply guessing. See how many of the big expense categories you can estimate—rent or mortgage payments, groceries, travel, contributions, meals in restaurants, tuition or child care, liquor, clothing, and of course interest, which we have already estimated. If the expenses estimated from the accounts for more than 70 percent of the total change in your working capital, you've done very well, and probably can work with your estimates to cut expenses.

Betty, though, could think of barely $27,000 in expenses, 57 percent of what she actually spent. So she did keep track of every penny for a couple of weeks, to get more information to improve her estimate. In the process she remembered whole categories of expense she had forgotten (her daily coffee from Starbucks at $2.47 added up to over $600 a year!). If she could do it, you can do it. If, after trying, you're still not sure where your money goes, you probably need to get someone—a competent friend or a reputable pro—to help you.

You need to learn where your spending hot spots are. Where do you spend money that you don't need to spend? With Betty, it was clear: when she feels stressed or low, she eats at restaurants. Other people buy clothes or books or gardening supplies or furniture. A cocktail every evening with your spouse can cost $1,000 a year!

You may decide that some of your spending vices are worth keeping; that choice is up to you. But if your credit cards don't get paid off and your retirement funds don't grow, at least you will know why.

The Cost of Borrowing

If you live on borrowed money, you will pay a lot of interest. A huge industry devotes itself to persuading people that the most important thing about a loan is the monthly payment. This is a lie: the most important thing about a loan is the rate of interest. Big payments are good, because they get you out of debt faster than small ones do.

How much interest are you paying on your loans and credit cards? Credit cards and credit lines generally charge anywhere from 16 to 21 percent. Mortgages and auto loans run about 7 percent, plus or minus 2 or

3 percent. Your rates may vary, and if this book is more than a year old, even the general ranges will have changed. So you will have to look at each loan's paperwork and find the annual percentage rate, or APR. The APR appears conspicuously somewhere on the original loan papers you signed and (in the case of credit cards) on each monthly bill.[4]

If you have a mortgage loan that required an up-front payment (called "points"), the APR takes that payment into account as part of the interest on the loan. That makes sense as a way of disclosing the real cost of the loan to someone thinking about borrowing, but since you already paid the points, they're sunk, like the money you lost in last night's poker game, and shouldn't enter into your decision making now. So for our purposes now, use the interest rate on the loan itself, not the APR. If you multiply the current balance of each loan by its interest rate, and divide by 12, you'll see how much you're spending per month on interest. Youch! Here's how the calculation looked when Betty did it:

Table 2.5

Rev. Dr. Elizabeth Grable
Working Capital Report
November 2000-01

	Annual Interest rate	2001	Monthly interest
LIABILITIES			
MasterCard	19%	$ 1,300	21
Nordstrom's card	15.5%	252	3
Checking line of credit	21%	4,200	74
Seminary loans	6.75%	18,200	102
Taxes due Jan. 15, 2002	0%	840	0
Loan on Corolla	7%	8,000	47
Morgage on 39 Rodeo Dr.	8%	192,300	1,282
TOTAL		**$ 225,092**	**1,528**

This figure was a surprise to Betty, as it is to most people. Interest of $1,528 a month, with compounding, is over $19,000 per year—a big chad punched out of a preacher's salary. Even leaving aside the mortgage interest, which is tax deductible and takes the place of rent, paying $246 a month (or, compounded, over $3,000 a year) is not good. That is real money you pay out in cash each month. Cut whatever costs you need to cut to make this outlay stop as soon as you can. The best strategy is to pay off high interest rate loans first; that way, you'll reduce your debt as quickly as possible.

(Some readers may wonder how I can say that Betty is paying $2,918 "per year" in interest on her credit cards when she didn't keep track of her interest expense for a whole year. Good point. The culprit is that little word "per." We can say that Betty is driving her car at 50 miles per hour even if she never drives as far as 50 miles or as long as an hour. Her speedometer says 50 miles "per hour," meaning that she would go 50 miles if she continued at that speed for a full hour. But she's going 50 now. In the same sense, we can say that Betty's MasterCard is socking her for 19 percent or $247 "per year" even if she plans to pay it off tomorrow. The real rate is something like 1.5 percent per month, but that's more math than I want to get into in this book!)

A good financial goal is to arrive at a point of paying off any credit cards in full each month and paying no interest on them at all. Probably this means getting rid of all but one or two cards; for many people it means cutting up all credit cards and going on the wagon. If, after two or three tries, you cannot make serious progress toward this goal, you need help. In many communities, nonprofit credit bureaus offer coaching for people trying to get out of debt. Remember: every dollar you don't spend in interest is money you can spend or save or give away. Getting out of debt is not a form of self-denial; it is a way to reclaim money for yourself that now is disappearing from your life.

The Ups and Downs of Investment

If your retirement money is in good long-term investments, it will go either up or down each year. Betty's net worth took a tumble this year because she had invested her retirement savings in stock funds. She could have avoided the decline by putting the money into a money-market fund.

With rare exceptions, money-market funds go only up; they pay interest, just like a bank account. This choice would have felt much safer, but it would have been a worse idea. Why? Because secure, fixed-income investments almost always grow more slowly than inflation. Over 10 or 20 years, money in a money-market fund can be expected to lose buying power, as inflation eats up value faster than the interest can replace it. "Safe" investments are good for the short run—a money-market fund is a great place to put the money you plan to spend on a down payment next November—but terrible for the long run. It is the wrong place to put retirement money.

To protect your long-term savings from inflation, you have to accept the up-and-down motions of the market. Risk, in other words, goes with higher long-term rewards. So grit your teeth and hang on to the roller coaster. The U.S. stock market has consistently rewarded those who buy a broad portfolio of stocks and hold onto them through thick and thin. Bonds (which are IOUs from corporations) go up and down a little less, but they also pay less, over the long haul, than stocks. The bond market has a history of moving up when stocks go down, and vice versa. Like a tightrope walker's pole, this tendency helps to stabilize your whole portfolio. The best retirement portfolio, for the great majority of investors, is a carefully chosen mix of stocks and bonds.

The best way to invest, for small investors, is through mutual funds, which pool money from a lot of small investors. Because the fund has a large amount of money, it can afford to hire professional managers and—most important—to spread its investments among many different stocks. With such a mix, a drop in one stock might be counterbalanced by a rise in others. Suppose, for example, that General Motors had big safety problems—bad publicity, government-ordered recalls, and product-liability lawsuits. That would tend to drive GM stock down. But a large mutual fund would likely also own shares of Chrysler, Ford, and Toyota. People who didn't buy GM cars would buy them from those companies instead, so those shares would go up. You can buy mutual funds either directly or through your denominational pension fund.

The worst thing you can do is to buy stocks (or stock funds) when the market is doing well and sell them when it's doing poorly. When you read about a "bull" market in the paper, that does not mean you should buy in. On the contrary, it means stocks are selling at high prices. Would you buy clothes at a store that advertised high prices? Smart people buy stocks when prices are low, hoping they'll be high tomorrow. The trouble is, no one is that smart. "Timing the market" is a foolish hobby. The best strategy is to buy stock mutual funds when your savings goal is in the distant future and buy safer investments, like bond or money-market funds, when you are going to need the money soon.

The most important investment decision you will make is how much of your money to invest in stocks and how much in bonds. Studies show that picking the right mix of "asset classes" is between two and nine times as important as picking the right stocks or bonds. If you are 45 or under, your retirement money should be almost entirely in stocks. As you get older, you should move money into corporate bonds, but not too quickly. If you are 55 and expect to live to 80, the midpoint of your retirement is still more than 20 years away, so most of your retirement savings are still long-term. At any age, money you expect to need within a year or two belongs in a money-market fund or, for nearly total safety, a certificate of deposit bought from a bank, credit union, or stockbroker.

One rule of thumb that many advisors suggest is to subtract your age from 110. The difference is the percentage of your money that should be in stocks. If you're 10 years old, you should put your money totally in stocks; if you're 50, you should have 60 percent in stocks and 40 percent bonds. In my opinion this division is too cautious; I would put long-term savings into stocks right up to 10 or 15 years before I planned to spend the money—this would mean leaving it in stocks until age 50 if you're going to retire at 65. You may be more cautious than I am, and that's fine. The main thing is to keep a substantial portion of your long-term savings in a stock fund where it will be likely to grow faster than inflation.

(Some advisors say that if you can't sleep at night, you have too much money in stocks. I say most people have far too little money in stocks, and should find some less costly way to sleep.)

Look at the statements from your pension, IRA, or other retirement accounts. Are your savings invested appropriately for your age? If you need to make a change, contact your retirement plan or mutual fund company and arrange a gradual move into the best investments for your age and goals. If you are going to move $10,000 from one kind of investment to another, it is best to do it one or two thousand at a time on a regular schedule, so you don't end up moving it all at a freak moment when the price of what you're selling is way down and what you're buying is way up. This strategy (called "dollar-cost averaging") is good whenever you plan to move much money from one kind of investment to another.

After you get your money into the right kind of investments, forget about it. Pay attention to your life, and remember that the Dow is not the Tao. Ignore it, and ignore the NASDAQ and the S&P 500, too. This attitude is hard for many people, especially those who brag the most about their stock-market exploits during the social hour after services. Not even the professionals can often beat the proven strategy of investing wisely, adjusting every year or two, and hanging tight when the financial headlines get exciting.

Start Early

If you start saving for retirement now, you will retire richer than if you wait. If you are 25, you're going to like this section. Every dollar you save today, given a modest 7 percent annual investment return, will, 40 years from now when you retire, be worth nearly $15. The trouble is, inflation will have eaten up most of the increase. If inflation averages 5 percent, the buying power of that $15 will be just over $2. So how do you figure out how much you need to save? Your denomination probably says 15 percent, your congregation (if it pays the bill) may say 10 percent or even 0 percent. How do you decide?

The field of retirement planning is complex enough to daunt even people who enjoy this kind of thing, so I am going to do my best to cut through the thicket for you. We all know that inflation, over time, reduces the value of a dollar: in 1955, when I was your age (assuming you were born yesterday), you could buy lunch at a lunch counter for a dollar. You could take piano lessons from my mom for two dollars a lesson, and my dad, who had a pretty good job, made $7,000 a year.

Thinking about money in the past or future requires adjusting the figures by some estimate of inflation. The most common estimate is the consumer price index, put out every year by the U.S. Department of Labor. According to the CPI, a dollar in 1955 bought about as much as $6.50 now, or, as the codger playing pinochle on the courthouse steps might say it, the dollar nowadays is worth just 15 cents (one dollar divided by 6.50).

I am going to take inflation out of the picture by using today's dollar as the standard. If I say you need $500,000 to retire, I'll mean you need enough of whatever currency people will be using in the future to buy what $500,000 buys today. That may be $7 million, or it may be 40 million pesos or 6 trillion yen—I don't care: I'll call it $500,000, and you'll know what I mean. It's 500,000 of what an economist would call "real" or "constant" dollars.

Likewise, if I talk about earning 3 percent on your investments, I will mean earning enough to make up for inflation, plus 3 percent. You may need to average a 7 percent or 10 percent return to achieve this; we'll still call it 3 percent because that's how much your buying power will grow. Economists call this growth in buying power "real return."

OK, how much should you save this year? That depends on many facts and assumptions: your age, how much you have saved for retirement already, how much you expect to earn on your investments, when you plan to retire, how much you think you'll need to live on in retirement, and when you plan to die. Who knows? All we can do is to make reasonable assumptions, and test whether our retirement savings would be enough to take care of us.

Here are some assumptions that seem reasonable, or even a bit pessimistic: You will retire at 65 and die at 85. Your investments will earn 5 percent more than inflation until you retire, and 3 percent after that. (Remember, as you get older you will move your money out of stocks and into bonds, which will go up and down less, but earn less on average.) After you retire, you will need 75 percent of your current income from your retirement fund, in addition to any income you may have from social security or other sources.

The following table estimates how large a percentage of your income you need to save each year from now until you retire. Across the bottom, find the number indicating how many times your current income you have saved already for retirement, and on the left, select your age. A 25-year-old beginning in the ministry with nothing saved who puts 15 percent of salary and housing into a retirement fund from now until retirement can expect— by this extremely rough approximation—to be able to retire in comfort.

Table 2.6

Percentage of your current income you need to save each year to produce 75% of your current salary between ages 65 and 85

Your Age	0	1	2	3	4	5	6
25	15	5					
26	15	6					
27	16	7					
28	17	8					
29	18	8					
30	18	9					
31	19	10	1				
32	20	11	2				
33	21	12	3				
34	22	13	4				
35	23	14	5				
36	25	16	6				
37	26	17	8				
38	27	18	9				
39	29	20	10	1			
40	31	21	12	3			
41	32	23	14	4			
42	34	25	15	6			
43	37	27	17	8			
44	39	29	19	10			
45	42	32	22	12	2		
46	44	34	24	14	4		
47	48	37	27	17	7		
48	51	41	30	20	9		
49	55	45	34	23	12	1	
50	60	49	38	26	15	4	
51	65	54	42	31	19	7	
52	71	59	47	35	23	11	
53	79	66	53	41	28	15	3
54	87	74	60	47	34	20	7
55	97	83	69	55	40	26	12
56	110	95	79	64	49	33	18
57	125	109	92	76	59	42	26
58	146	127	109	91	72	54	35
59	173	152	131	110	90	69	48
60	210	186	162	138	114	90	66
61	267	238	209	180	150	121	92
62	361	324	286	249	211	174	136
63	550	495	441	387	332	278	224
64	1116	1011	906	801	696	591	486

How many times your current salary you have saved for retirement now

For the Rev. Dr. Betty, the chart has a more troubling tale to tell. She has $62,400 saved for retirement—1.25 times her $50,000 income, so she chooses the column labeled "1," because that is the closest to 1.25. Betty is 48, so she selects that row. I hope she is sitting down when she reads across and finds the number 41, meaning that in order to retire she'll have to save 41 percent of her income from now till then. This is a shock, but it's an important shock to have this year instead of five years in the future, when (if nothing changes) she would have to save 66 percent.

Many middle-aged clergy, faced with facts like these, throw their hands up and declare that it would be impossible to save this much. But think about it—if you can't live on 60 percent of your income now, how do you think you're going to live on less than that when you retire? At some point it will be necessary to cut down on your spending. Better to cut down sharply now than to retire in poverty.

The table is correct mathematically, but depends on many assumptions. It ignores any equity you may have in your home, and it assumes no increases in your income during your career, beyond cost-of-living raises. Many people now retire at 70 instead of 65—this change alone would reduce Betty's 41 percent to a more manageable 22 percent. There is nothing magical about the notion that you'll need 75 percent of your current income when you retire. You may want to spend more after you retire!

The most uncertain assumption of all is that your investments will earn 5 percent more than inflation. Three percent is a cautious guess—between 1925 and 1998, stocks returned an income closer to 7 percent above inflation; even bonds earned something like 2 percent.[5] Of course, higher income from investments helps a young person much more than an older one. The older you are, the greater the risk that the years between now and retirement will happen to be the worst in stock market history. If you are past your midlife crisis, stick with my cautious 5 percent estimate, and for good measure, save a little more than the table says you should.

We've now filled up the back of a good-sized envelope with your current money situation. Whether you were pleased or shocked by the result, keep it in mind as we begin to think about the values questions lurking behind the financial ones. And don't worry. You can talk and even preach about money issues even if your own financial house is not in perfect order!

Resources for Further Learning

The financial snapshot in this chapter is only the beginning. If you want to learn more, seek out some of my favorite books and other resources:

Personal Finance

One of the most challenging books on personal finance is *Your Money or Your Life*, by Joe Dominguez and Vicki Robin (New York: Penguin, 1992). This book and the small movement it has inspired show that it is possible to spend radically less to have more time for unpaid pursuits.

David Bach takes a somewhat more conventional approach in *Smart Women Finish Rich: Seven Steps to Achieving Financial Security* (New York: Broadway Books, 1999). Bach has a wonderful way of asking startling questions, such as "What does money mean to you?"

Superstar financial advisor Suze Orman earns her pay (well, maybe a hundredth of it) by giving comprehensive, clear, reliable advice. You'll find sound, conventional views and quite a bit more about the details of buying individual stocks than you need to know, written in a smooth, accessible question-and-answer style, in her modestly titled *The Road to Wealth: A Comprehensive Guide to Your Money* (New York: Riverhead Books, 2001).

Investing and Retirement Planning

The only investment guide you'll ever need is *The Only Investment Guide You'll Ever Need* (New York: Harvest, 1999) by Andrew Tobias. With irreverent wit, Tobias will inoculate you against the most common financial scams, while proving that the best investment of all may be a case of tuna fish.

The only other investment guide you'll ever need is Amy Domini's *Socially Responsible Investing: Making a Difference and Making Money* (Chicago: Dearborn Trade, 2001). Domini is one of the most influential experts on socially responsible investing, and her readable guide will give you the basic knowledge you need to bring you portfolio into line with your beliefs.

If you want to follow my advice and invest in mutual funds rather than directly in stocks, a good primer is *Smart Money Moves: Mutual Fund Investing from Scratch* by James Lowell (New York: Penguin, 2000).

If you don't like the assumptions built into my retirement savings table, many retirement-planning tools are on the Internet. One of the best is the "Ballpark Estimate," maintained by the American Savings Education Council at *www.asec.org*. If you want to play around and learn the consequences of possible decisions about saving for retirement, the Ballpark Estimate will let you adjust the assumptions. The ASEC site has more financial calculators than Radio Shack, all of them free.

Career Planning

Finally, if this chapter (or your last board meeting) inspires you to consider leaving the clergy life, you may find it helpful to read James Hightower and Craig Gilliam's book *A Time for Change: Revisioning Your Call* (Bethesda: Alban, 2000).

If you're simply thinking about moving to a new position, you can find help in James Antal's *Considering a New Call: Ethical and Spiritual Challenges for Clergy* (Bethesda: Alban, 2000).

CHAPTER 3

Money as a
Spiritual Challenge

*It is not the man who has too little who is poor, but the one
who hankers after more. What difference does it make how
much there is laid away in a man's safe or in his barns, how
many head of stock he grazes or how much capital he puts
out at interest, if he is always after what is another's and only
counts what he has yet to get, never what he has already. You
ask what is the proper limit to a person's wealth? First, having
what is essential, and second, having what is enough.*

Seneca
Letters to Lucilius

If the work of the preceding chapter was especially painful for you, you
do not need to be convinced that money can oppress the human spirit.
In this chapter we will explore this possibility a little further, and also
look at the positive potential of a spiritual life that embraces the challenge
of money while placing ultimate trust elsewhere.

Money is a spiritual challenge because it arouses great depths of passion
in us and requires the best of us in moral reasoning and courage. The most
exquisite acts of charity and the most heinous acts of cruelty have this in
common: money is the most frequent medium through which the act is
done. The most soul-destroying vices and the most ennobling spiritual
disciplines both require "free" time, which in our society costs money. What
excuse can we have for skittering around the subject, or for dealing with it
superficially, in a house of worship?

Money is a medium of power through which we act and are acted upon. A spiritual life that does not concern itself with money can have little effect on our daily lives, especially in a culture as saturated by financial forces as ours. Strong feelings about money threaten to preoccupy us: shame at lacking it, pride in having it, fear of losing it, compulsive eagerness to spend it, gluttonous delight in hoarding it. Each of these feelings has a moral and spiritual dimension: At worst, shame can render us unconscious of our kinship with God's family; pride can make us feel like gods ourselves. Fear can take away the courage requisite for moral action. Compulsive spending, like compulsive hoarding, turns our attention toward ourselves and away from the well-being of others. At its best, though, money can be a spiritual plus. Money earned for useful work is an encouraging symbol of our worthiness and value. The thoughtful use of money—spending, saving, investing, giving—is an effective way to care for others and realize our visions of a better world.

Despite the spiritual importance of money, clergy and congregations often speak of it simplistically, or only in connection with our own personal or institutional needs. Those needs are large; the institutional machinery of U.S. religious life costs far more per capita than in any other country. Like all other institutions in this country, American religious groups deal with money constantly—all the more reason we should focus actively on the whole range of spiritual challenges money raises, lest the inadvertent message be that faith has nothing more to say than "Gimme." To accomplish this aim, we need to understand and overcome the silence that surrounds money in so many synagogues and churches.

Sources of Clergy Reticence

One reason for our silence is that clergy—who, more than anybody else, decide what will be talked about in congregations—have special challenges where money is concerned. Some of these blocks are personal. In school, many of us shunned fields of study that involved too many numbers. Consequently, some of us approach any quantitative topic with disinclination, distaste, even phobia. Practical money management does not, in fact, involve much math beyond simple arithmetic, but sometimes "math anxiety" keeps us from even trying. Most math-anxious people are much smarter about math than they think. The anxiety most often has its beginning during junior high school, where some students (many of them boys) begin to excel in math, while others (often girls) decide that they can't do it. As an adult you probably have outgrown many negative aspects of your junior-high self-image. You can overcome this one, too.

Another block for clergy, discussed in chapter 2, is that if our personal finances are not well organized, leadership and teaching about money can be awkward for us. It is not necessary to solve all of your financial problems (no one ever does), but it helps a great deal to be aware of the state of your finances and to have a financial plan. If personal finances are a source of anxiety for you, it is important to make progress at home while you are exploring the spiritual side of money with your congregation.

Systemic Barriers

Clergy reticence to engage congregations about money is not simply a matter of personal failing. Part of the problem is built into the structure of our congregations. One clue that the difficulty is partly systemic is that clergy across the spectrum find it hard to ask for reimbursements, raises, parsonage repairs, and other ordinary outlays. This is partly a function of personal awkwardness, which can express itself either in too weak or too forceful self-assertion. But behind the awkwardness is something structural: it is hard to ask for money because of role conflicts built into our dealings with the congregations we serve. It is hard to claim our due from lay leaders at whose funeral we might officiate, and it is hard, after a conflict over money, for the treasurer to invite us into an embarrassing family situation involving her 16-year-old child. In the end, too many clergy avoid financial conflicts by neglecting to ask for what they need, trusting that lay leaders will do what is right. In the long run, this can be a costly strategy, both in dollars and in our effectiveness as leaders.

No one finds it easy to ask for a raise (why else would this theme appear so often in cartoons?), but it is especially difficult for clergy to advocate for ourselves in our financial relationships with our congregations. A young rabbi at a workshop said:

When I was hired, it said in my contract that the temple would buy me a PalmPilot. Someone on the board thought I should have it, and I wanted one, so they put it in. Five years later I still haven't gotten it. I could go out and buy it and give them the bill, but somehow I just haven't. It's a small budget as it is, and $400 might mean we'd have to cut the youth director or some other program. Also, after so much time has passed, I know that if I did it now, someone would say, "Why does a rabbi need to carry a computer?"

Paralyzed by his sense of responsibility for the synagogue and its youth, this rabbi may be hurting both by failing to hold lay leaders accountable for their promises.

In theory, episcopal and presbyterian polities clarify the roles of laity and clergy by making the clergy leader accountable to a regional church body rather than to the congregation. But in practice, money for the local ministry almost always comes from local people. In the United States, those who pay the piper normally expect to call the tune, which leads them to think of clergy leaders as employees—a role in tension with the roles of teacher, pastoral caregiver, and spiritual leader.

Like elected politicians, clergy are expected to lead the very people on whom they depend for their livelihood. But unlike politicians, most clergy feel inhibited from openly campaigning or fund raising for themselves. People expect clergy, and we expect ourselves, to be compassionate and nonjudgmental and continually on tap in case of need. It is hard to shift from this need-meeting role to become a strong self-advocate or even to claim what the congregation has already agreed to.

I believe that these problems will persist so long as "meeting the needs of members" remains the tacit mission of most congregations. This definition comes naturally to Americans, because so many other institutions define their purpose this way—serve the customer, fulfill client expectations, meet a need. Even congregations whose official mission statement points outward—to serving the community, spreading the gospel, or challenging the status quo—easily fall into the consumer frame of mind unless the outward focus is actively reinforced by teaching and example. Only then can the mindset shift from "service for a fee" to covenant for ministry, in which laity and clergy serve together.

Theological Dualism

Clergy shy away from talking about money not only for personal and structural reasons but also for theological reasons. Clergy reticence is often abetted by a tacit dualism that calls money secular and therefore separates it from the sacred. A related dualism assigns leadership in "spiritual" matters to clergy and in "secular" concerns to laity. In one national survey, more than two-thirds of the respondents agreed with the statement that "money is one thing; morals and values are completely separate."[1] In consequence, the clergy voice is often silent about money questions.

Faith-money dualism has little to do with scripture or tradition, nor does it accord with our daily experience. A central affirmation of the biblical tradition is that God created one world and declared it "good."[2] Enjoyment of prosperity is often portrayed, as in this passage from the Book of Exodus, as a reward from God:

> For the Lord your God is bringing you into a good land, a land with flowing streams, with springs and underground waters welling up in valleys and hills, a land of wheat and barley, of vines and fig trees and pomegranates, a land of olive trees and honey, a land where you may eat bread without scarcity, where you will lack nothing, a land whose stones are iron and from whose hills you may mine copper. You shall eat your fill and bless the Lord your God for the good land that he has given you.[3]

There is no denigration of wealth or consumption here. Note, however, that the "you" to whom the land is given is a plural "you." God is rewarding the whole people, not individuals; God's covenant is with the community. The accompanying warning, too, is for the people as a group:

> Do not say to yourselves, "My power and the might of my own hand have gotten me this wealth." But remember the Lord your God, for it is he who gives you power to get wealth, so that he may confirm his covenant that he swore to your ancestors, as he is doing today.[4]

This passage describes wealth as a gift of God in covenant with a "stubborn"[5] people, conditioned on their obedience to God's commandments. It follows that the right use of wealth, also, will be oriented outward to community, rather than inward to the self.

The prophets pronounced special condemnation on those who become wealthy through injustice:

Because they sell the righteous for silver
and the needy for a pair of sandals—
they who trample the head of the poor in to the dust of the earth,
and push the afflicted out of the way . . .[6]

The point is not that money or personal wealth or even self-indulgence is a bad thing, but, as theologian Carol Johnston put it, that "wealth brings with it the danger of a desire to cling to it for its own sake, rather than use it freely for the sake of the larger community."[7] Far from a dualism of the spiritual and financial sides of life, the teaching here is that our choices about wealth and money occupy a central place in God's vision for humanity.

Our everyday experience confirms a strong connection between faith and money. Money plays a central role in virtually all important ethical decisions. The way we earn and spend and give away our money during our lives shapes in large part the memories we leave behind. Money may not in itself be sacred, but when we approach the sacred in our lifetime, money almost always is nearby. "One who wishes to acquire wisdom should study the way that money works," wrote Rabbi Yishmael in the Talmud, "for there is no greater area of Torah-study than this."[8]

Jesus' teachings about money are notoriously hard to summarize—he challenges one man to give all of his wealth to the poor,[9] praises another for giving away only half of his,[10] and at yet another time, scolds his disciples for proposing to sell some "very costly ointment" to give to the poor, instead allowing it to be poured onto his head. Jesus then brushes the disciples off with seeming indifference: "[Y]ou always have the poor with you, and you can show kindness to them whenever you wish, but you will not always have me."[11] Christian theologian Sondra Ely Wheeler has concluded that because the role of money in the modern world has changed so much, the New Testament cannot give us "concrete rules" about how Christians should manage wealth, or even "ethical principles with a clear and fixed application."[12] Jesus seems instead to be challenging his listeners one by one to consider expressing a new quality of commitment to God and to other people through their use of money. In this respect, he stands in the broad biblical tradition described above, which varies in particulars but consistently sees choices about wealth and money as deeply reflective of our ultimate commitments.

By excluding money from the spiritual sphere, a congregation squanders an important part of its potential to change lives. By growing in assurance with respect to money and treating the subject as belonging to the religious sphere, clergy can begin to banish false dualisms and share more fully with the laity in leading the whole congregation.

Positive Thinking

Having criticized the dualist theology that walls off spiritual life from money, I should add that another long-standing, trans-denominational, and interfaith trend in American religion takes almost the opposite approach. French traveler Alexis de Tocqueville, listening to preachers in the young republic, found it "difficult to ascertain from their discourses whether the principal object of religion is to procure eternal felicity in the next world or prosperity in this."[13] No doubt he meant this statement as a criticism, but some preachers would happily accept his description. In the years immediately before and after 1900, Baptist journalist and minister Russell Conwell preached a "Gospel of Wealth," part of whose message was that "it is your Christian duty to get rich!"[14] At about the same time, inspirational writer Ralph Waldo Trine urged readers to achieve "Peace, Power, and Plenty" by getting "In Tune with the Infinite." God, Trine taught, continually gives life by way of a "divine inflow" that we need only accept. Humanity and God are one in essence, and different only as a drop of water differs from the ocean. When we accept God's inflow, we receive happiness, health, and material prosperity along with it. It is up to us:

> If one hold himself in the thought of poverty, he will be poor, and the chances are that he will remain in poverty. If he hold himself, whatever his present conditions may be, continually in the thought of prosperity, he sets into operation forces that will sooner or later bring him into prosperous conditions.[15]

Trine reduces the distance between God and humanity, of which Calvinism makes so much, almost to zero. Our spiritual task is simply to accept what is and to enjoy the benefits.

Trine's influence was great and lasting, and inspired many others. During the Great Depression, World War II, and afterward, the pastor-writer Norman Vincent Peale taught a similar viewpoint as *The Power of Positive Thinking*.[16] In our time, innumerable versions of "abundance" or "prosperity" theology carry on in the same vein. The idea that human wealth (along with human health and happiness) is high on God's list of priorities has never enjoyed strong support from academic theologians or mainstream denominational bodies. From at least the days of Job, the deeper writers on religion have frowned on this cheery kind of faith. The idea that God wishes us as individuals to become wealthy with no ethical or covenantal strings attached is out of tune with much of the biblical text. Nonetheless, theologies that simplistically equate wealth with divine favor remain tempting, especially in this country, to people with wealth and—what is perhaps more difficult to understand—to those who lack wealth but hope one day to get it.

It would be hard to overstate the influence on American thinking of this broad impulse—which is part of the even broader phenomenon that Yale historian Sydney E. Ahlstrom called "harmonial religion." Many lay Christians, even in churches where the clergy teach otherwise, believe that God will reward them financially for their faith and good behavior. There is scarcely a congregation in America, regardless of its stated creed, that is not influenced to some degree by these ideas.

You can probably raise more money for your congregation by fusing faith and money than by separating them into compartments; but both approaches sidestep many of the spiritual challenges money presents in daily life. If God wants me to be rich, how does that help me to decide between a job that pays well and one that offers a more relaxed lifestyle? If God rewards a cheerful giver, will God also help me to decide which of the charity appeals in today's mail I should contribute to, and how to balance charitable giving against paying child support or saving for retirement? Can I rely entirely on God to pay my credit cards, or are there other things I should be doing? If God decides who will be rich, how should I understand the poverty around the world, and how should I respond? A simplistic marriage of religion and finance is little better spiritually than a complete divorce, because neither extreme—compartmentalizing faith from money or co-opting faith in money's service—addresses the deeper challenges of life with money.

Polarities

What does it mean to have a spiritually mature relationship with money? One thing it means, certainly, is to face facts rather than denying or distorting them. Having sketched, in chapter 2, the broad outlines of your money situation, you have taken an important first step. Spiritual maturity also means taking account of reality in all its paradox and ambiguity, rather than resorting to quick doctrinal fixes. Decision making about money does not lend itself to pat ethical formulas. Short of renouncing money for a life of poverty (which is even harder than it sounds), we cannot escape the need to balance multiple, sometimes conflicting values. Generosity, as good as it is, stands in tension with our other obligations—to care for our families, to take responsibility for ourselves, to deal fairly with others in the marketplace. No doubt most of us could and should be more generous than we are. At the same time, though, we could invest more of our money in constructive business ventures, provide more adequately for our retirement, and care better for our dependents—which may or may not involve providing more money for them. A spiritually mature person balances competing values, not for the sake of compromise but to "hold fast to what is good"[17] even when ends refuse to meet.

A useful way of looking at pairs of competing values is to see them as polarities. Organizational consultant Barry Johnson has developed a method he calls "Polarity Management," which treats opposite tendencies or values not as problems to be solved but as polarities to manage.

> Polarities to manage are sets of opposites which can't function well independently. Because the two sides of a polarity are interdependent, you cannot choose one as a "solution" and neglect the other. The objective of the Polarity Management perspective is to get the best of both opposites while avoiding the limits of each.[18]

Analysis of a polarity requires looking at both the advantages and disadvantages of each side—not to weigh them against each other or to strike a compromise, but to understand the dialectic between values that both have something positive, as well as something not so positive, to offer. One polarity important for a spiritual approach to money pits having time against earning money.

Having a Career—Having a Life

Benjamin Franklin's aphorism "Time is money" is usually taken to mean that we should look for ways to do things quickly, because if we do them slowly, we "lose" time that could be spent productively—that is, in earning money. But this interpretation makes sense only from the standpoint of the part of life we call "work." In the rest of life, the part we call "personal life" or simply "life," time is not a commodity to be sold, but a thing of value in itself. The difference between having a career and having a life is not that one is more sacred or more worthy, more fun or more difficult than the other. It is the different role of money that distinguishes these goals. Career time is obligated time; having a career means—usually, though not always—earning money. Having a life means having "free" time—time for taking pleasure, doing good, creating value for yourself and others. Ideally, we could achieve both at once; in reality, most people hold them in a complex and sometimes desperate tension.

We have a career to earn money. If we learn to need less money by needing fewer material goods or buying what we need more cheaply, we can spend more of our time as we wish. No one has put this point more eloquently than Henry David Thoreau. From his retreat at Walden Pond, Thoreau watched men build a railroad track from Boston. On its way west, the track passed close by Walden Pond, as it does today. A friend, knowing that Thoreau loved to travel, urged him to take the train to Fitchburg. "But I am wiser than that," wrote Thoreau:

> I have learned that the swiftest traveler is he that goes afoot. Suppose we try who will get there first. The distance is thirty miles; the fare ninety cents. That is almost a day's wages. I remember when wages were sixty cents a day for laborers on this very road. Well, I start now on foot, and get there before night. . . . You will in the meanwhile have earned your fare, and arrive there some time tomorrow, or possibly this evening. . . . And so, if the railroad reached around the world, I think I should keep ahead of you.[19]

Thoreau highlights an error that is still widespread: we forget how much of our time goes to earning money to buy goods and services whose value consists in—saving time!

Thoreau's critique applies to many economic choices. Shall I book another weekend day to conduct a wedding ceremony? Yes, I will, because I'm saving money for my family to go on a summer vacation. The vacation is important because I will have time to spend with my children, who don't see much of me because, as a minister, I work weekends. Thoreau took an extreme position, going all the way in favor of having a life and against having a career. Contradicting Genesis, he wrote, "It is not necessary that a man should earn his living by the sweat of his brow, unless he sweats easier than I do."[20]

To such dilemmas there is no obvious right answer, but it should be clear that in the context of such choices time is definitely not money. Rather, time and money are two poles of a single value system that might be diagrammed this way:

Table 3.1

	Having a career	Having a life
+	Economic security Prestige Power Choices Toys	Family life Friendships Play Curiosity-driven learning Flexibility
−	Job stress Emptiness of money as a goal Loss of personal identity Proliferation of material "needs" Loss of friendships	Anonymity Lack of the power only work can give Loss of adult identity Going without Debt

I have filled the boxes with positive and negative aspects that occur to me; you may wish to make your own list, by yourself or with a group. Within a polarity, relationships are dialectical: when you commit to too much career time, work becomes overwork, and soon the negatives on the left side predominate. You start to dream of cutting back, living more cheaply, and retiring early. If you free up too much time (as many retirees do), the negatives begin after a while to outweigh the positives. This situation motivates you to seek the upper half of the left side of the polarity—poverty or boredom can be a spur to work.

Like any polarity, this one isolates a single aspect of a complex system. Many variables affect our choices about work and leisure—the wage rate we can command, the special needs of those we love, the intrinsic satisfaction of our job, and our native health and energy, to name a few. This polarity assumes freedom of choice about work and leisure—a luxury by global standards, but one more available to affluent Americans than we sometimes admit.

Many Americans experience the downside of this polarity—some because they are unemployed or underemployed, others because they are overworked. Part of the pressure for Americans to overwork comes from employers, for whom it is more economical to have fewer workers working long hours than more workers working short ones. But this practice is not new. Why can employers now demand almost a month more work per year from their employees than they could in 1947?

One reason, surely, is the escalating expectations of consumers for more, larger, and better-quality goods. To buy these things, you need more money, and if longer hours are the price, you pay. Another reason is that many people who identify strongly with their jobs live in and for them. The workplace becomes an ersatz home, their coworkers an ersatz family.

Clergy can't sidestep this polarity. I would once have been inclined to sidestep this issue as affecting me. I'd have said, "My career is different. The ministry is a calling; I don't do it for the money, so this polarity doesn't apply to me." My attitude changed one day when I was working on my sermon. The phone rang; I picked it up. It was church business, and I dealt with it. When I hung up, my wife was angry. "I never mind it when they call you at night because somebody dies or has an accident. I don't mind the evening appointments; that's your job. What I can't stand is when you're working on your sermon, I'm not supposed to bother you, the kids aren't supposed to bother you, but the phone rings and you talk to *them*." It was a lesson for me: however much like real life my job felt to me, my real, *real* life was waiting for me—patiently or not—at home.

Balance. The spiritual issue here is one of balance: "For everything there is a season, and a time for every matter under heaven." Ecclesiastes continues:

What gain have the workers from their toil? I have seen the business God has given to everyone to be busy with. . . . I know that there is nothing better for them than to be happy and enjoy themselves as long as they live; moreover, it is God's gift that all should eat and drink and take pleasure in all their toil.[21]

Work, in this perspective, is no all-consuming vocation. It is simply "the business God has given to everyone to be busy with." Work has its place, play has its place, and wisdom consists in maintaining a reasonable alternation. Ecclesiastes, to be sure, stands at the laid-back end of the scriptural continuum. Our stories of faith also include heroic toilers like St. Jerome and too many martyrs to count. Each of us has to choose, in the light of our best self-knowledge and deepest discernment of the good, what kind of "balance" we are called to.

Self-denial—Self-indulgence

A second polarity involves self-denial and self-indulgence. Religious people from the dawn of history have sought to focus their attention and deepen their spiritual lives through practices of self-denial. Muslims fast in the daytime during Ramadan; Jews avoid leavened bread during Passover. Catholic priests vow celibacy; Buddhists and Hindus practice vegetarianism. Perhaps the most universal form of self-denial is the practice of keeping silent, briefly or for days, to create an empty space in which to feel the presence of the sacred. In our time and country, where overindulgence is so great a part of our way of life, it is not surprising that some of these practices have seen a modest revival.

In some of the world's religious traditions, Christianity and Buddhism especially, one option has been to take up the monastic life. In theory, monasticism should simplify the matter; the monastic way is, if not to relinquish money altogether, then at least not to pause too long from prayer or meditation to grasp after it.

Of course, in practice, even monasteries have to make a living, and in the United States, the begging bowl is not a widely understood approach to fund raising. I once attended a seminar for national religious leaders at the Menninger Clinic about psychiatric problems in the clergy. Bishops, abbots, and denominational staff members came to learn how to deal with clergy who have come unhinged. During the breaks, most of us cast about for topics of mutual interest—but not the abbots. They talked with each other about recipes for the fruitcake and preserves sold by their communities! There is no way to escape the tension between God and mammon.

In the United States, the truly cloistered spiritual life has not caught on with large numbers of people, even among clergy. The idea of a pastor who spends life in quiet study, prayer, and contemplation exists mostly as a romantic notion. The real life of a religious leader—I don't need to tell you—combines association management, social work, and politics; too often, study, prayer, and contemplation drop out of the clergy plan book. Like it or not, the clergy life is a life of engagement. For us, as for our congregants, the ascetic life must be, at most, a sometime thing. The popularity of Zen Buddhism in the United States is based partly, I think, on the wish of people whose lives are consumed with the modern samsara wheel of "get and spend" to step back and consider letting go of some of their attachments. Zen schools and monasteries have developed great skill over centuries at making the insights of nuns and monks available to lay Zen students.

Deliberate self-denial is a timely spiritual practice in a country where three-quarters of the people live more opulently than the Buddha, even in his days as Prince Gautama, could have imagined. But self-denial is not the only practice favored by religious wisdom; self-indulgence gets its due as well. Religious holidays are the most obvious example of "holy excess," or consumption in the service of spiritual insight. The New England Puritans frowned on Christmas, both because of its roots in the "pagan" festival of Saturnalia and because it was so often celebrated, as the Rev. Increase Mather said in 1687, "in Compotations, in Interludes, at Cards, in Revellings, in excess of Wine, in mad Mirth."[22] Such comments give some support to the idea of Puritanism as "the suspicion that somewhere someone might be having fun." But even the Puritans observed feast days, one of which we have inherited, indirectly and with many changes, as Thanksgiving.

Sacrifice and Feasting

Self-denial and self-indulgence are not opposites; their relationship is paradoxical. Of this the most vivid illustration is the first ritual attested in the written history of religion, and one of the most widespread: the sacrifice. The world's oldest scriptures, the Vedas, first chanted some 3,000 years ago in ancient India, are largely concerned with sacrifices to the gods. In the sacrifice, food was laid on the altar, where the altar flame, representing the fire-god Agni, "consumed" sacrifices and carried them to the recipient god.[23] The hope was that the gods would grant a boon, either of good fortune or of inner transformation. These themes—the gift to God in the hope God will reciprocate, and the transformation of the inner life of the worshiper—have remained widespread in sacrificial worship through its many permutations.

The Vedic gods to whom a sacrifice was given did not always keep it for themselves. Often the food was eaten by the priests and worshipers, as well as by other gods, in a sacrificial feast. The Temple sacrifices detailed in the Book of Leviticus sometimes include such sharing. Only the "burnt offerings" of livestock or poultry required the priest to burn most of the offering "into smoke," retaining only a little for himself. In other types of sacrifice, the proportions are reversed: only a token amount is burned, and the rest either "belongs to Aaron and his sons" (that is, the priests), or is enjoyed as a sacrificial meal by offerer, family, and friends. The offering is given entirely to God, but God responds by hosting a celebratory meal.[24] The passages usually cited in support of tithing refer to this kind of sacrifice. Two out of three years the tithe is sacrificed, then eaten by the family that gives it. On the third year it is sacrificed, then given to "the Levites . . . the resident aliens, the orphans, and the widows."[25]

The Christian sacrificial meal, the Eucharist, follows a similar pattern. Originally worshipers brought bread and other products of their labor to the altar during the offertory to be used in the ceremony; today in most churches money serves that function. (In some Christian traditions "offertory" still refers primarily not to the collection of money but to the eucharistic bread and wine brought to the altar by laity, the bread on occasion baked by a worshiper). The priest "offers" the bread and wine symbolically, re-enacting Jesus' self-sacrifice, and then shares them with the congregation. Give, and then receive; sacrifice, then feast. Self-denial is to self-indulgence as inhaling to exhaling, or as prayer to action. Giving sacrifice to God betokens faith that one's own daily needs will be supplied in turn.

When I was a teenager, I had a liturgical idea that I have yet to summon the courage to enact. My fantasy was to collect the offering as usual, have the ushers bring the baskets forward, sing the Doxology and say the blessing, and then set the offering on fire. The appeal of this for me, of course, was that it would expose my elders' hypocritical materialism. At the very least, it would immediately distinguish those who put cash into the plate from those who gave by check!

More seriously, burning the offering would put a bright spotlight on the anomaly of money playing such a prominent role in worship. To many people, the offering plate is somewhat embarrassing—and in some affluent churches it has been dispensed with as unseemly. (Synagogues traditionally do not take up a collection during services, not because money is unkosher but because handling money is a form of work, and therefore forbidden during Shabbat.) Money, in a religious context, raises for many people the painful issue of their own self-indulgence. By inviting gifts, churches ask a question that the wider culture does not ask: Do I have money simply to buy things for myself, or are there higher purposes to which some of my wealth might be committed?

For most people, including clergy, the polarity of self-indulgence and self-denial comes to this: How can I live a faithful life in a world that is so much engaged in getting, spending, and accumulating money, given that I am not ready to abandon that world altogether? And for clergy as congregational leaders, it is this: In a culture where desire is checked only by bank balances and credit limits, how can we help people to gain perspective on their own consumption and the social structures that encourage it? Given that most Americans could scale down their consumption greatly before suffering harm, where is the happy medium? Neither self-indulgence nor self-denial is all bad or all good; again, they are related as a polarity:

Table 3.2

	Self-indulgence	Self-denial
+	Joy in life Appreciation of God's world Sharing with friends and family Makes faith appealing	Look inward, not outward, for joy Detachment from material things Simple life Freedom from distraction
-	Self-centeredness Addiction Greed Idolatry of sensual experience Neglect of responsibilities toward others	Imposing denial on others Depression Self-harm Idolatry of ascetic experience Making faith unattractive

The ritual of sacrifice embraces both sides of this polarity—in giving and receiving we experience both God's demands on us and God's bounty for us, the discipline of loosening our grasp on our possessions, and the joy of receiving as a gift the spiritual and material things we need.

Control—Trust

One of the most frequent images Protestants use when talking about money is "stewardship." Religious sociologist James Hudnut-Beumler has defined stewardship as "the responsive practice of human beings tending to what has been placed in their care by God."[26] This image, which alludes to Jesus' parables of the good and unjust stewards,[27] was popularized between 1900 and 1910 by a group of denominational leaders.[28] Until recently, the word "stewardship" was rarely used outside Protestant churches, and mostly in connection with raising funds. Church leaders customarily insist that they are talking about stewardship of "time and talent," as well as "treasure." Nonetheless, one church member in five understandably defines the word to mean "Giving a certain percentage of your money to the church."[29] More recently the stewardship idea has been adopted by some Roman Catholics, and even by the management consultant Peter Block, who defines it (strangely, I think) as "accountability without control or compliance."[30]

Given such a broad range of meanings, it is not surprising that, as Robert Wuthnow observed:

> [S]tewardship is not meaningful to most Americans—or even to many churchgoers. And stewardship, when it is discussed, is presented in so many different guises that people can interpret it pretty much as they like. When they do so, moreover, they prefer vague understandings that make little difference to how they should behave from day to day.[31]

The continuing appeal of stewardship to clergy and lay leaders stems from the conviction that all that we have is "placed in our care by God." Not everyone holds this belief by any means; indeed, the concept is so countercultural that it is a strain even for those who believe it theoretically to imagine what acting on it would mean. But in a time when we have grown more aware of the bad effects of human management of the world's resources, the idea of a higher accountability is timely. Stewardship retains its appeal precisely because it is countercultural, and advocates a spiritual stance that holds us accountable to something greater than ourselves as individuals or even as a species.

Religion has not always helped humanity to feel accountable for our use of the world's resources. A biblical image that has come under strong criticism lately is God's command that Adam and Eve should "fill the earth and subdue it; and have dominion over the fish of the sea and over the birds of the air and over every living thing that moves upon the earth."[32] To modern sensibilities, this passage describes only too well what has occurred. Humanity has spread over the earth, depleting and polluting resources and causing other species to become extinct at an unprecedented rate. It is easy to see our species as "bad stewards" who have used our master's wealth unwisely, diminishing instead of adding to it. But this very criticism presupposes our dominion—or at least enormous power—over the earth. And with power comes the responsibility of care.

Stewardship implies a world in which humans manage God's resources. But alongside stewardship—and somewhat in tension with it—is the thought that we should trust in God's abundant generosity. When the Israelites complain of hunger in the desert, God gives them manna to eat, but cautions them through Moses not to gather more of it than they need each day, because tomorrow more will come.[33] In a similar vein, Jesus, faced with a hungry crowd of his own, encourages his disciples to share what they have. Whether by a miracle or by the power of example, there turns out to be enough for the 5,000 and to spare.[34] The trust here is not in human stewardship but in a God who watches every sparrow and adorns the lilies to outshine "Solomon in all his glory."[35] Such total trust in God is very different from the spiritual standpoint of the steward, on whom God depends. The trust we feel as God's children and the control we exercise as God's stewards form a polarity:

Table 3.3

	Control	Trust
+	Resource conservation Prudent stewardship Conscious planning Saving for times of scarcity	Resource sharing Gains from prudent risk-taking Joy in spontaneous consumption Freedom from worry
−	Selfish accumulation Obsessive money management Needless self-denial Unwillingness to share decision making Excessive risk-avoidance Missed opportunities	Resource waste and destruction Losses from reckless risk taking Excessive spending Overdependence on others

The question, then, is how to balance faith in God's ultimate intention for us, and the realization that, at least from our finite point of view, a great deal depends on our own efforts. In many congregations, people approach this question differently depending on how they earn their living. Civil servants, teachers, and others whose salaries are paid reliably by large, stable institutions are apt to be confident of the future but unaccustomed to taking risks. Corporate workers who daily face the risk of being laid off for reasons unrelated to their competence or loyalty may come to feel that efforts at control are futile. Business owners, as a group, spend much of their time controlling their firms' finances, but understand that great accomplishments always require risk. Actions that may look to others like sheer gambling are, to the entrepreneur, an act of faith both in one's own ability and in larger forces of the marketplace.

There can be no final answer, but in respectful conversation it is possible to move beyond the false sense of certainty and moral condescension that so often surrounds questions of control and trust.

Spending—Saving—Giving

After taking stock of your own values, you can do essentially three things with money: spend it, save it, or give it away. Aside from having it stolen or flushing it down the toilet, that's about it. Religious institutions understandably encourage giving; every congregation broadcasts at least one message about money and morality: "You should give some of it to us." Unfortunately this statement often is all people hear. Such a limited message does not, needless to say, reflect the best religious thinking. It is not effective even at raising money, because it does not begin to touch the delicate balance of desire, anxiety, and obligation that go into even the simplest choice among the options: spending, saving, or giving.

From the clergy point of view, it is all too easy to notice and decry the lavish lives some people lead, especially those who plead poverty when asked to support the congregation. We are less apt to know about the irresponsibility of those, including some of our "best" givers, who do not prepare for sudden unemployment, who do not save for their retirement, or who fail to insure their children's health when they could do so. The moral choices people face in managing their money are complex, not simple.

Spending

To a visitor from elsewhere, one of the most striking features of life in the United States is the quantity of goods Americans own and use. This is not a new trend. Thorstein Veblen, one of the most influential critics of American consumption, wrote about the new rich of the late 19th century. These wealthy industrialists' material needs were satisfied, but they spent and consumed ever more opulently to achieve the admiration and envy of others. This was done through what Veblen called "conspicuous consumption," which served the wealthy as a "means of reputability." Such consumption, he wrote, "must be an expenditure of superfluities. In order to be reputable, it must be wasteful. No merit would accrue from the consumption of the bare necessities of life."[36]

Veblen's observation rings true today, not only for successive generations of *nouveaux riches*, but for Americans of other economic classes also. The "Veblen effect," whereby "consumers are willing to pay a higher price for functionally equivalent goods" because they are thought to be used by people of higher status, is well known to marketers.[37] This tendency is the rationale behind celebrity endorsements. It also powers the success, especially since the 1980s, of "premium" ice cream, "quality" pens, "designer" clothes, and other goods that command a higher price than functionally identical products on the basis of imputed prestige. Increasingly, high price itself has become the mark of a preferred product:

In virtually every product category, there was an item or brand that proudly, even defiantly, set out to be more expensive than all others. This brand, almost by definition, would then become the standard of "taste" and "quality" against which less esteemed items could be measured. No one seemed to notice that a basic tenet of market capitalism was being turned upside down: Price was dictating value, rather than vice versa.[38]

In a striking study of the Veblen effect, economist Srully Blotnick asked 181 returning vacationers how satisfying their trips had been. After recording their answers, he told half of them that "someone rich and/or famous" had stayed in the same town or hotel. Asked the same question two weeks later, members of this group raised their estimate of the trip's satisfaction value by 43 percent, while the control group's memories had dimmed by 6 percent. The Veblen effect distorts our perceptions even when we buy investments; many people buy tax shelters or tax-free municipal bonds even when they are not in a high enough tax bracket to make up for the low returns on such securities.[39] Clearly the desire to appear affluent or to identify with those who are remains a powerful engine behind our country's famous overspending.

On the other hand, we Americans have long criticized ourselves for excessive materialism. Veblen's *Theory of the Leisure Class* is only one of many popular jeremiads against overspending. In recent years, this self-criticism has increased, even as our taste in sneakers, cars, and restaurants has grown more refined. The irony has not escaped observers. Sociologist Robert Wuthnow notes that "[t]he American public voices concern about the reign of materialism in our society while wandering the corridors of the mall."[40] Our self-criticism has an anguish in it, like the repentance of a drinking alcoholic: we know that it is hard to reconcile our habits of behavior with our highest aspirations for ourselves.

Opinion polls confirm the gap between values and behavior—or perhaps it would be better to say the gap between one set of values and another. In a 1992 survey of 2,000 members of the U.S. labor force, Wuthnow found that 89 percent agreed that "our society is much too materialistic," 74 percent said, "I wish I had more money than I do," and 76 percent named "having a beautiful home, a new car, and other nice things" among their most important values.[41] No doubt some people have reduced their consumption to be less materialistic, and probably more have adjusted their philosophy of life to fit their behavior. But those in the overlap—the ones who criticize materialism while admitting they are part of the problem—consciously experience a painful tension that affects most of us at least unconsciously. We question the prevailing materialistic ethos, but we contradict ourselves, not only in our actions but also in our beliefs. One person buys a gas-guzzling sport utility vehicle, reasoning that her family's safety is more important than fuel economy, while another righteously spends an extra $10,000–$15,000 for a hybrid car that gets 80 miles per gallon. Either way, consumption is defended by a moral argument. My point is not that one decision is correct (you already know the answer to that question) but that our deliberations about spending are not simply a matter of thrift versus extravagance. For us, consumption is not merely an addiction; it is one of the chief ways we express our values.

The great spiritual challenge, where spending is concerned, is to develop a personal sense of "enough," so that with the Passover song, we can say dayenu—"it is sufficient." This effort is partly a matter of taking an honest look at our real motives for spending, partly of learning to feel more strongly the competing claims of saving and giving.

Saving

American ambivalence about spending is matched by ambivalence about accumulating wealth. While our rates of consumption are unmatched, however, our savings rate is lower than that of citizens of most other wealthy countries. Saving—the effort to build wealth—competes with consumption, and often loses. We sometimes think of wealth and consumption together. As Veblen observed, consumption functions as a symbol of wealth. But in reality, for most people wealth and consumption are naturally opposed— those in too much of a hurry to live like the rich never get there. The rich themselves often live strikingly frugal lives. There is a great difference, in this regard, between those who have built their own fortunes and those who have inherited their wealth. The distinctive mark of the self-made wealthy is not income but frugality. One study, for example, found that the typical "million-heir" spends nearly twice as much on suits as other millionaires. This is not to say that one can become rich by spending less on suits; but certainly many people who earn enough to accumulate considerable wealth choose instead to spend their incomes. Meanwhile others whose incomes are more modest become wealthy by living doggedly below their means and investing the difference.[42]

Suspicion of the Rich

Americans assume that everyone wants to become rich, but at the same time we suspect that wealth brings its owners into moral peril. Alongside our acquisitive traits is a strong tradition, especially among poor and middle-class Americans, of suspecting that the rich have achieved their status by questionable means, or that they are corrupted by their wealth.

This mixed attitude toward wealth is reflected in American fiction. The hero of Horatio Alger's late 19th-century novels—always a young man who rises "from rags to riches"—represents one side of the dichotomy. Born poor and virtuous, he ascends through his own efforts to wealth and fame—but along the way encounters and resists many temptations that would distract him from his goal. The implication is that wealth is acquired through a combination of persistence and virtue. On the other hand, heroes like Mark Twain's Huckleberry Finn represent the idea that poverty is the natural milieu of common-sense morality, while the spurious morality of the powerful is a mask for self-interest.

Even the desire to be wealthy, while virtually universal, is tempered by the sense that one might have to be grasping or dishonest to achieve it. Robert Wuthnow, in a 1992 opinion survey, found that 71 percent of the American labor force agreed that "Being greedy is a sin against God." Even more—87 percent—of those who called themselves weekly churchgoers agreed with that statement. Smaller proportions (46 percent and 51 percent) agreed that "Money is the root of all evil."[43]

Such ambivalence complicates any effort to achieve a spiritually balanced attitude toward saving. How do we distinguish prudence from miserliness? Clergy who are aware of the complexities can help people make good judgments about saving. When Joseph interpreted the Pharaoh's dream about the seven fat years followed by the seven lean, he was putting Egypt's prosperity into the larger perspective of a world in which no nation is exempt from trouble. Putting one-fifth of each year's produce into storage probably struck his advisors as extremely overcautious. How about other uses for that wealth? How about the poor, the priests, the infrastructure? There are always noble reasons not to save (and self-indulgent ones as well). But Joseph could provide, as one speaking for a God whose vantage far exceeded Pharaoh's, a longer-term perspective. By Joseph's higher mathematics, a 20 percent savings rate seemed reasonable, especially in a world without stock markets and compound returns.

Giving

Clergy will be much more persuasive asking people to give when they understand that giving is not always the superior choice. A family's charitable giving should fit into its whole financial situation. Once a man stood up in church to pledge a large gift to the capital campaign. The church needed the money, and he felt good about his giving, his prestige and influence as a lead donor, and the gratitude he received. His minister, however, knew that this man had recently gone to court to have his child support reduced because his income was too small—too small, that is, to support both children and a lifestyle that included a late-model sports car, a beachfront condominium, and overseas vacations. In this perspective, his pledge, while not bad in itself, lost much of its moral luster.

While too many congregations never mention money except to ask for it, too few congregations do a good job of asking for money. I think these two facts are deeply connected. In our hearts we know we have not done the spiritual work with people that we need to do to help them to make sound decisions about giving. And for the most part we have not done the same work for ourselves. I will have more to say about advocating for generosity in a future chapter; for the moment, let us look at how a congregation might begin to do that preparatory work.

Working on the Spiritual Challenges of Money

One of the most poignant images from the conversations I have had with clergy as I wrote this book is that of a man who, for eight months, got up every morning, donned a suit and tie, and took the train to Boston, so that people in his suburb wouldn't know he had been laid off from his job. The members of his church, sadly, were among those from whom he kept his secret. What a gift it would have been had he belonged to a congregation where the ups and downs of economic life were advertised among the spiritual crises it would be OK to talk about!

How can we as clergy leaders help to create such congregations? First, I think it is important to shed the sense of certainty with which we are tempted to clothe ourselves, especially when we feel uncertain. That is why I have chosen in this chapter to present the spiritual challenges of money not as problems for which I have solutions, but as dilemmas for which no one has a final answer. Every person who seeks to live well must manage these dilemmas continually. With clouded moral sensitivity and finite knowledge we make choices, knowing that our choices will never be exempt from criticism.

Congregations vary greatly in their willingness to meddle in the personal choices of their members. When sociologist Sharon Miller compared four congregations in a midwestern city, two (Mennonite and Assemblies of God) frequently heard sermons urging them to question the prevailing cultural emphasis on consumption, and invited members into small-group settings to consider personal finance and lifestyle issues. The Catholic and Presbyterian churches, on the other hand, observed a prudish silence about money except during the fall pledge drive.[44] Any effort to open up the subject of spirituality and money will need to begin where the congregation is and move from there.

Some traditions authorize their clergy to give leadership about money. Some strict congregations actually prescribe rules for personal finance. Sectarian or radical groups expect clergy to encourage a dissenting stance in a world whose values are understood to be "other." Clergy leaders in such settings have a mandate to engage people on economic and financial issues. Most of my experience is in congregations that give little such permission. In such congregations, talking about money when not strictly necessary can spark resistance, even condemnation.

But it is not only congregations that resist talking about money. Most of us clergy collude in our congregations' reticence oftener than we challenge it, perhaps because we underestimate our power to influence people. I had a shock one Sunday years ago, a week after preaching a sermon titled "Letting Go." My point was that our lives are full of attachments that feel virtuous and indispensable, but when we adopt a wider spiritual viewpoint we may find that we are called not to hold fast but to let go. The following Sunday a middle-aged woman shook my hand during the social hour and said, "I thought about your sermon, and this week I took your advice and quit my job!" Clergy who deliberately set out to preach about money challenges often are surprised at people's openness to challenging ideas.

Ministry offers many opportunities to raise money issues. Many clergy invite engaged couples to discuss their sexual relationship, not only because sexual adjustment is important to the success of a marriage, but because we see the sexual and spiritual as two aspects of a whole. Why not ask them to talk about the financial side of the relationship as well? Likewise, when there is a death, a family has to deal not only with grief but also with inheritance and other changes in their money resources. Not every family will respond to an invitation to explore the spiritual meanings of these changes, but that's no reason not to extend one. I routinely offer to accompany families to their meeting with the funeral director. My presence not only helps to limit the expense but also allows me to see how various funeral directors deal with customers, so that I can advise people in the choice of a funeral home.

Pastoral care and counseling, public and private prayer, religious education for adults and children, and many other moments offer opportunities to express care and concern about the money issues people face. The barrier, oftener than not, is our own timidity as clergy. I have tried to offer a framework for raising questions about faith and money that does not presume the authority to prescribe answers or take for granted that the congregation is prepared to set itself against the larger culture.

In a cartoon an older priest lecturing a younger colleague says, "There are two topics you should always avoid in preaching: politics and religion." No doubt any clergy leader who insists on raising awkward (or to put it differently, important) topics will inspire resistance, even outrage. Those signs simply mean that you have people's attention. Count instead the countless people, some of whom resist the loudest, to whose urgent spiritual challenges you could be speaking.

CHAPTER 4

Congregations Considered Economically

What you are in charge of is not a community of faith but a business enterprise. Your seminary professors do not understand this. Seminary professors are very short on knowledge of how a local church operates, few of them ever having been pastors, but your bishop understands it. The trustees or board or vestry or session of your church understands it. Your brother clergymen understand it. And your wife, who must cope with the frequently grim facts of parsonage economics, understands it. (You may be amazed at the rapidity with which she grasps the essential nature of the church.)

Charles Merrill Smith,
How to Be a Bishop without Being Religious

One of the more irritating refrains heard regularly in synagogue and church board meetings is this:

LAYPERSON: This congregation needs to run more like a business. It is a business, after all.

CLERGYPERSON: But we're not a business. We're not here to make a profit.

This conversation has all the freshness of a prayer-book versicle and the information content of a sun-dried mushroom, and it contains many levels of misunderstanding.

It assumes that there is one way to run a congregation "like a business." But businesses are run in many ways. In my first congregation, in Boca

Raton, Florida, many lay leaders fell into one of three groups: retired entrepreneurs, Florida Atlantic University professors, and IBM employees. I expected the professors, whose idea of management was to appoint study committees, to come into conflict with the entrepreneurs, who were used to making quick and unilateral decisions. What surprised me was how different the entrepreneurs were from the IBMers. In a large company like IBM, middle-management authority is given to those who have expertise and a good track record, not to those who have a personal investment in the firm. The decision process is slow and deliberate—routinely millions of dollars are spent exploring possibilities that never happen. And middle managers are much more likely to be spending a budget than walking the tightrope of investment, sales, operating loans, payroll, and cash flow that is the daily fare of the small-business owner. The IBMers, in their propensity for deliberation, resembled the professors, not the entrepreneurs. There is no one way to run a congregation "like a business" because there is no one way to run a business.

Nonetheless, the demand that the congregation "run more like a business" makes clergy feel uncomfortable, for at least three reasons:

It is a challenge to our competence. "This congregation needs to run more like a business" might be translated, "My professional skills are relevant and useful here and yours are not; stand back and defer." Never mind that the speaker is more apt to be a motor-vehicle inspector or a botany professor than a business owner. Such comments sometimes are spoken in revenge by people who have been made to feel religiously incompetent. If the clergyperson feels economically incompetent, as many of us do, the challenge finds its mark, and our anxiety is raised.

It undermines the values that motivate good churchcraft.[1] This effect is indirect. In business, the accepted motivating value for both entrepreneurs and workers is to make money. Indeed, modern capitalism sometimes wraps itself in an ideology that terms the unfettered pursuit of material self-interest "rational." Other motives—duty, generosity, idealism, or adherence to tradition—become "irrational" by implication. Philanthropy becomes a hobby, religion becomes recreation, and community becomes at best a form of infrastructure for achieving aims deemed rational. Only the pursuit of profit is a central goal of life. Suggesting that a congregation ought to emulate a business reflects and reinforces our culture's suspicion that religious enterprises have little value of their own.

It has some truth in it. No matter how strongly we believe that the congregation is concerned with people and religious values, we know that it is also an economic entity that must manage personnel, real estate, equipment, cash, investments, and debt. We know that somehow we should do this "religiously," but it's not clear just how our finance or personnel committee meetings ought to be different from such meetings at Microsoft or the Humane Society. More unsettling is that we're not sure exactly how the role of clergy leader ought to differ from that of corporate manager.

We don't want the congregation to become a business, but we'd like it to be as efficient and effective as we imagine business to be, and many of us wouldn't mind if our pay took a baby step toward those excessive CEO salaries we've read about. The purpose of this chapter is to introduce some of the key concepts economists and business experts use in thinking about business firms, and to show how they do or don't apply to congregations.

Ownership and Mission

A for-profit corporation begins life with an investment. One or more investors pool their money and create the corporation, which issues them stock certificates. The stockholders elect a board of directors, which elects top managers, who hire the rest of the employees. Investors organize this way, instead of simply owning the business as individuals or as a partnership, because businesses have to borrow money. If an unincorporated business borrows money and can't pay it back, the owner or partners have to satisfy the debt. But corporate stockholders are protected from a corporation's debts.[2] This protection stems from an important technicality: it is the corporation, not the stockholders, borrowing the money. Stock values can decline to zero, but not below. This makes corporations much more daring about borrowing and taking business risks than individuals would be if each were liable for the consequences. The corporation, invented during the 19th century, has been crucial to industrial development, because it allows business owners to amass the large sums necessary to build factories and other massive projects. Nonetheless, in the beginning it was a novelty and looked to many like a scam. *Utopia Limited*, a Gilbert and Sullivan operetta, parodied the British Joint Stock Companies Act of 1862 this way:

Some seven men form an Association,
(If possible, all Peers and Baronets)
They start off with a public declaration
To what extent they mean to pay their debts.[3]

It is easy to see how the corporation seemed to be simply one more way for business owners to get rich—as, of course, many did. But the large enterprises corporations made possible also led to an increase in wealth for the working and middle classes. Every society that wants to share in that increase has had to allow people to form corporations or some near equivalent.

A typical church or synagogue is also a corporation, but a special kind called "not-for-profit" or "nonprofit."[4] Like a business corporation, a nonprofit has a governing board, which may or may not be elected by a larger membership. Board members enjoy partial protection from personal liability similar to that allowed to corporate directors in a business,[5] and the corporation operates under a charter from the state. Because of the First Amendment to the U.S. Constitution, religious corporations have considerable latitude in the details of their organization, and the courts are reluctant to impose themselves on their internal governance. But basic corporate rights, including the right to own property, to sue, and to be sued, are granted by the state.

Incidentally, it may seem odd to think of a "right" to be sued. But think about it: what could you do, economically, if you couldn't be sued? You couldn't borrow money, except maybe from your mother, because the lender would have no recourse if you didn't pay. It would be a hazard to let you drive a motor vehicle, because anyone you injured would have no way of getting reimbursed. You would be like a child too young to sign a binding contract. Since there would be no way to compel you to keep your side of the agreement, few would want to risk it.

An incorporated congregation is in all these ways much like a business corporation. But in other ways it is quite different. As nonprofits, congregations don't have "owners." They and their property are held in trust by—you guessed it—the board of trustees. (This group may go by various names according to the congregation's polity, but every state requires that there be one body designated as the ultimate governing board of an incorporated congregation.) My father, who served for many years as a church trustee, frequently stressed the point that it was the corporation—not the members or trustees as individuals—that owned the church's property. I recalled those words when, as a teenager, I served a term as a trustee of the same church. One night late, my girlfriend and I were parked in the church lot, using it for strictly private purposes. I remembered my father's lesson when a police officer shined his flashlight into the car and asked sarcastically, "You two members of the church, are you?"

The stock in a business corporation is the stockholders' property, and the company serves their financial interests by making money. Technically, the directors are fiduciaries for the stockholders, who are beneficiaries. This means that the directors must act in the stockholders' best interest, and (theoretically) may not act contrary to that interest. The governing board of a congregation is in a different position. Membership in a congregation (or other nonprofit corporation) is not property, and the corporate body is forbidden to serve the individual financial interests of its members. In particular it may not give any of its property to members, even when it dissolves. It can pay reasonable salaries or fees to people who are trustees or board members, but these must be based on work performed; if they resemble the "dividends" paid by a for-profit corporation, the nonprofit status of the congregation may be at risk.[6]

Who, then, owns a congregation? One answer would be that like all corporations, it owns itself—even stockholders own only their shares, not the corporation or its assets. But on a more practical level, it is the mission, as set forth in the corporate charter and then clarified by the organization itself, that "owns" the congregation. Just as directors of a business corporation serve the interests of the stockholders, nonprofit trustees serve their corporation's purpose. Even when members of the congregation meet to make decisions, they act not for themselves as individuals, but in behalf of the congregation's purposes. This legal situation fits the theology of many congregations, which hold that the "owner" actually is God, and that members and leaders ought to act not on their own desires, but on God's will as best they can discern it.

Managing Capital

For all the differences between for-profit businesses and congregations, some economic concepts from the business world can be useful to us as we manage what has been entrusted to us. One is the idea of capital. Capital assets include land, buildings, and machinery—the enduring property used by a business. "Working capital" includes the corporation's cash, securities, and other more liquid forms of wealth. Capital, along with raw materials and labor, is what the company uses to produce goods and services.

A company's original capital (that is, the money used to purchase capital assets) is contributed by its first stockholders; later it may raise additional capital by issuing new shares of stock, by borrowing from banks or individuals, or by investing some of its profits. All of the providers of capital—stockholders, bondholders, and banks—expect a fair return, and so the more capital a company has, the more profit it needs to make to repay its investors. Even when it invests its own earnings, the company does so at the expense of stockholders, who would otherwise have been entitled to receive them as dividends. Every dollar's worth of capital a company has is contributed by someone who expects to be paid for the use of the money.

Banks and bondholders are paid interest for their contributions. Stockholders can be paid in two ways—either through dividends or by increases in the price of the stock. A company that produces profits is attractive to investors, who know that even if it retains and reinvests all of its earnings, their share of the company's value will increase. One way or another, capital has to be paid for annually.

The cost of capital imposes a discipline on business. It ensures that property will be used profitably. A company that only "breaks even" on its business operations every year is really losing money, because it cannot pay for the capital it uses. In time, its factory and equipment will be repossessed by the bank and creditors, or stockholders will replace its management with executives who can run the company profitably enough to repay them for their investment.

Congregations, too, use capital—an important fact too many congregations ignore. We hold land, buildings, equipment, and endowments. The "investors" who contributed a congregation's capital do not demand interest or dividends; many of them may be dead. Nonetheless, the congregation owes its investors a return on capital—not in the form of profits, but in the form of mission. When donors give to a building or endowment fund, they do so in the expectation that their money will help to fulfill the congregation's mission every year from then on. This is a moral obligation on which a congregation can default more easily than a business can stiff its investors.

One way of looking at the cost of capital is through the economic concept of opportunity cost. If you put $1 million under a mattress when you could have invested it and earned 5 percent, you do not "break even."[7] You lose the opportunity to earn $50,000 a year. That is the opportunity cost of your decision. Likewise, a congregation with a building worth $1 million incurs an opportunity cost of around $50,000 a year before it even opens its doors.

This idea came into play when I consulted with a regional judicatory in a denomination that was suffering membership decline. The leaders realized that to reverse the trend, they needed to start new congregations, so they asked me to do a presentation about how to do that. As I laid out the realities of congregation planting—the need to recruit and train clergy and then subsidize them in the field—the leaders' faces fell. They realized that even a modest new-congregations program would cost several hundred thousand dollars; this was more than they could imagine raising from their demoralized membership. I asked them whether the judicatory owned any property. Yes, it owned a seaside conference center that "broke even" every year, but the property was estimated to be worth more than $5 million. I pointed out that it was costing $250,000 a year not to sell the conference center property. Was it worth that much to have a conference center?

The judicatory's situation was, economically speaking, the same as if it had $5 million in endowment and was paying $250,000 to lease the conference center. In that case, would the judicatory continue to subsidize the conference center? Probably not. Its leaders would see the money flowing in and flowing out, and they would ask themselves, "Could we fulfill our mission better by spending $250,000 in some other way?"

Businesses have to ask this question about all of their capital assets because their mission is to make a profit, and if they don't get an adequate return on every dollar's worth of capital, in the long run they will go out of business. We religious leaders need to ask ourselves the same question, for the sake not of profit but of mission.

Another cost of capital, and especially of buildings, is accumulated wear and tear, which if not repaired immediately becomes deferred maintenance. Deferred maintenance is like an unpaid debt. Each year the roof goes unpatched or the exterior unpainted, the debt grows. Business accountants keep track of this debt by carrying depreciation as an accumulating liability. This method works pretty well for lathes and forklifts and less well for buildings, but at least it is a reminder that what looks like a break-even year may be much less than that if the growth of deferred maintenance is considered. Congregations oftener than not ignore this cost of capital until calamity befalls.

Considering the cost of capital is not merely a financial or accounting exercise. It is a necessity of prudent stewardship. Leaders of congregations often are entrusted with valuable property contributed by generous people in years past. We owe them a fair return on their investment—not in dollars, but in mission.

Managing People

Congregations, for all their variety, have in common some distinctive modes of people management, and for good reasons. Congregations also depend heavily on volunteers, who can quit at any time, so we need to pay constant attention to the nonpecuniary benefits of volunteering. Congregations depend on voluntary giving, so we need to know how to inspire active support of the mission from potential donors. And congregations serve human needs, which are by nature illimitable, so clergy, staff, and volunteers need to take responsibility for setting boundaries, saying no, and protecting themselves from stress and burnout.[8]

All that I have mentioned so far would be true of any nonprofit, but a congregation is yet more complex. In churches and synagogues, especially small ones, the constituent groups overlap. The board, stockholders, management, labor force, clients, volunteers, and donors are all drawn from the same pool. In this situation it can be a challenge to keep people motivated while maintaining discrete roles and boundaries.

Every paid staff member in a congregation has at least two major organizational relationships—to the staff team and to a natural constituency: the choir for the music director, parents for the educator, finance committee for the bookkeeper, and so on. More than in business, or even in a typical nonprofit, the staff members of a congregation need to manage both relationships to succeed. When employees favor one relationship and neglect the other, their effectiveness is compromised.

Especially in polities that give the congregation members a strong role in governance, staff members tend to tilt toward their constituency and away from the staff team and its leader. Boards and committees come to see themselves as "supervisors" of the employees with whom they work most closely. This system regularly fails, for several reasons. Committees cannot supervise staff effectively, because they do not speak with a united voice and are not present when the work is done. Consequently, a committee that becomes involved in the minutiae and emotional complexity of supervising staff fails not only as a supervisor but in its primary role as a planning, policy-making, and evaluating team.

Most serious of all, when staff members become one-sidedly connected to their various constituencies, the congregation's work is fragmented. In place of a systemwide pursuit of agreed-upon goals, fiefdoms develop, and staff members find themselves pursuing separate and sometimes conflicting goals. At worst, staff people can be pitted against each other on behalf of factions in the congregation. A staff team needs to recognize the power of the centrifugal forces that attempt to divide it; it also needs to be wise and energetic in maintaining a centripetal covenant among staff members to be united in pursuit of a common mission.

When the staff team tilts too far toward unity—for instance, when the clergy leader or administrator tries to be a rigidly hierarchical CEO—other problems develop. The staff must deal with natural constituents, many of whom also play other roles as clients, donors, workers, and stockholders, and need to be included in shaping the organization's vision and goals. Each congregation has to find its own way of striking a balance between maintaining a united staff team with a coherent sense of mission, and an open and participatory style of management within each program area.

Measuring Results

A central difference between congregations and for-profit businesses is that a congregation exists for reasons other than to make a profit. (Someone in the back row of the finance committee mutters, "You can say that again.") If not for profit, then for what? I would say, generically, that a congregation seeks to change the lives of human beings in ways that fit its charter purposes.[9] This kind of result is not nearly so easy to measure as a dollar profit, but it is not so hopelessly vague as to be exempt from any kind of quantification. Ideally, a congregation should be clear about whose life it hopes to change, and in what way, and it should reward its workers, paid and unpaid, when they contribute to that outcome.

The problem, then, is a widespread one: How do you measure results when your mission is to change lives, not to make money? Actually, the word "measure" is misleading; it implies that a thing matters only if we can assign a number to it. But in the congregational environment less than half of what matters can be quantified. As useful as attendance, pledge income, and the number of new members are, it is the qualitative aspect that is most important.

It is easy to say, "We confirmed 15 young people this fall." It's a little harder to set goals for the level of religious literacy you hope to challenge each of those young people to achieve. Such goals would need to be produced with the participation of staff, volunteers, parents, and young people. At best the result will lack the crispness of a numerical target. The best qualitative goals have some numbers mixed into them:

We will identify all of the 13- to 18-year-old children of church families, and give each of them two invitations—one from a peer, one from an adult—to participate in our youth program. The program will offer each participant a positive, drug- and alcohol-free social experience; four one-day retreats including opportunities for learning spiritual practices, studying the Bible at a college level, and creating a personal belief statement. Graduating seniors will be invited to read their belief statements during services. Our goal is for each participant to grow in religious literacy, sense of belonging to the church, and ability to apply biblical concepts to moral and ethical choices.

Having agreed on a goal statement like this, it becomes possible to tie the rewards for staff and volunteers, including youth leaders, to the goals. Instead of thanking people for the time and trouble they have taken, for example, we can thank them by describing—again, qualitatively—the way they have achieved the goal. In addition to counting heads at youth events, we can ask participants to set personal goals for themselves and evaluate, with peers and adult leaders, how they have progressed toward achieving them. If in the serendipity of time, something good happens that's not on the list, then we congratulate ourselves for achieving a creative variation on the goal!

Qualitative goals (like learning spiritual practices or growing in religious literacy) cannot be measured with mathematical precision. The evaluation will be verbal, not numerical. But it is a far cry from throwing up our hands and drifting from year to year, as many congregations do.

The idea of measuring results inspires strong resistance in many congregations because we tend to think that we achieve an important goal simply by existing. If your congregation's implicit mission is "To be the Methodist church on Main Street," or "To provide a Jewish education for our children," you are at risk of wasting scarce resources that could be used effectively. But if you define whose life you are going to change and how, and how you are going to know when you've succeeded, you can unite the contributions of your donors, staff, and volunteers, and earn the gratitude of the community you serve.

Distributing Rewards

A congregation's mission is to change lives. But in truth we are ambivalent about this goal, and rarely reward our lay and clergy leaders when they achieve it. Changing lives *also* effectively upsets the congregation's equilibrium and prompts efforts to revert to normal, often by ejecting the change agent. For clergy especially, the incentive is to go along and get along. When Ralph Waldo Emerson wrote, "The virtue in most request is conformity," one of the first illustrations that came to his mind was a minister:

> I hear a preacher announce for his text and topic the expediency of one of the institutions of his church. Do I not know beforehand that not possibly can he say a new and spontaneous word? Do I not know that with all this ostentation of examining the ground of his institution he will do no such thing? Do I not know he is pledged to himself not to look at but one side, the permitted side, not as a man but as a parish minister? He is a retained attorney, and these airs of the bench are the emptiest affectation.[10]

Emerson may be a bit unfair, but he has put his finger, as only an ex-cleric could, on the pressure we all feel not to rock the boat. We, and those who work under our leadership, are regularly punished for success at changing lives—but we can counter that by articulating the real mission of the congregation and rewarding those who contribute to fulfilling it.

This challenge is not unique to congregations. In recent decades, many businesses have learned that "profit for the shareholders" is an inadequate mission even for them. Profits excite shareholders, but companies need the best efforts of their other stakeholders—among them customers, workers, managers, and bankers—to succeed. To inspire this diverse group, many businesses have tried to state their mission in terms of the needs they hope to meet, the social changes they are aiming for, and the achievements they hope their workers will feel proud of. One of the problems companies encounter when they try to define their mission to transcend profit is that managers are ultimately rewarded or punished by shareholders, who care more than anybody else about the company's profitability. Consequently, other stakeholders may have reason to be cynical about the stated mission and the expectation that they help carry it out. Like congregations, such businesses, to make their mission credible, must rearrange the reward system of the company to reinforce it.

The great pitfall for congregations is that over time they fall into the habit of providing rewards willy-nilly, without reference to the mission. Old Mr. Johnson gave an endowment for the choir, to honor his late wife, Mildred, the soprano. Mr. Johnson receives considerable benefit from his gift; he feels each week that the choir is carrying Mildred's love of music forward. But Mr. Johnson is particular about the kind of music he appreciates; like the choir director, he prefers sacred music composed before standards declined in about 1800. When someone proposes something new, the question is not "Will this music help us to change lives?" but "How will Mr. Johnson feel about it?" By encouraging this question, the music director protects herself from having to learn new material and shifts responsibility for her limited effectiveness to Mr. Johnson.

This congregation has a vague, half-conscious sense of the mission of its music program, and consequently a haphazard reward system for those who support it. I know of no way to avoid this kind of situation altogether, but I know what helps. First and most important is an active planning process that articulates the mission of the church as it is expressed through music. Second, it helps to acknowledge frankly that donors, staff members, volunteers, and even clergy expect and are entitled to rewards for their contributions to the mission. In the case of donors, this concept is very different from the common attitude that donors benefit the congregation and ask nothing in return. Third, it helps to publish a "wish list" of contributions (in this example, gifts) that would advance the mission, and the rewards (naming opportunities, influence on program content, recognition, etc.) it is prepared to offer in exchange.

With these practices in place, someone probably would have asked Mr. Johnson directly whether one of the things he wanted in exchange for his gift was control over the music program. He probably would have said no. Or possibly he would have made his restriction explicit. And the congregation would have been empowered to say no, if his restriction would hinder its mission.

Another donor story: one member of my first church was a wealthy management consultant I'll call Ken. Once a year or so Ken came into my office and gave me an hour or two of free advice about the church. Ken was used to charging corporate leaders hundreds of dollars an hour, but for me he had a check in hand for 10 or 15 thousand, which he would give the church if we would follow his advice. I listened as patiently and respectfully as I could. Then I told him that I disagreed with his advice, and that in any case this was not how decisions were made in this church. Then he would leave. About half of the time he left the check behind. One day Ken happened to be singing my praises (this was not his only tune!), and I asked, "What is the secret of my success?" He was stumped for a minute, and then blurted, "You treat everyone—the same!" I am convinced that the church was one of the few places Ken could go where people would be honest with him, and that that was one of the rewards he gained for his many real and valuable contributions to the church.

It is not always obvious what people will regard as a reward; this is as true of staff and volunteers as it is of donors. Some rewards are relatively obvious—salary raises or bonuses, for instance. People also enjoy pleasant surroundings, congenial co-workers, and the chance to participate in institutional decision making. Many congregations could become more effective by accepting frankly that these desires are real, and working to become a more attractive workplace by rewarding their best workers well.

Some rewards for workers need to be handled carefully. We all know people who work in a congregation because it gives them a venue to avoid problems in their family or marriage, or to get extra pastoral care. Some of the best staff and volunteers work partly for such reasons, but it is both risky and unkind to exploit their needs. It is better, when we become aware of such unhealthy motives, to help them to find ways to meet their needs in more appropriate settings.

People can get all kinds of satisfaction out of working for or giving to a congregation. Some of the things people want are inappropriate. But by careful planning and management, we can reward contributions that support the mission and avoid rewarding those that impede it. Some people will respond by taking their contributions elsewhere, but not all. It is not the function of a congregation to give people everything they want; indeed, one of its central functions is to change what people want—to make them want new things. By stating a clear mission and acknowledging that people expect various kinds of rewards for their contributions, we can encourage gifts of money, energy, and time that help the congregation to change lives.

The argument over whether a congregation ought to be more like a business can be a productive one if everybody recognizes that there are two sides to it. Congregational leaders have much to learn from economists and business types about how to regard the money and capital assets we hold in trust. At the same time it is important to orient people in business (and other occupations) who come into lay leadership positions that the ways of doing things they learned at work may or may not apply to congregational life. A congregation is owned by its mission, not its members, and unlike businesses and most nonprofits, congregations cannot sort customers, stockholders, labor force, and management into neat, separate groups that can be led and managed and rewarded in distinct ways. That is why leading congregations is and always will be an art unto itself.

Advocating for Truthfulness

In the smoking room of the Yankees Club, Mr. Roxbury stubbed his cigar into a jade ashtray brought from China by one of the original tea barons of the 18th century. Business conversation was forbidden in this room, so Roxbury chose a topic from another realm entirely. "Wilson," he wheezed to the gentleman sitting to his left, "what do you think of Dr. Folsom, our new minister?"

Mr. Wilson cinched his smoking jacket and gazed thoughtfully at one of the many hunting trophies on the wall— the head of a tiger from the Bengal. "Impressive. Impressive in so many ways. Doctorates from Stanford, Oxford, Harvard. Fourteen books. A fine choice—reflects well on the church, that sort of thing."

Roxbury grunted his approval. "Yes, and it was right to decline the party's nomination. It wouldn't do to have a mayor of the cloth. Not the thing. Not the thing at all. Devoted to the ministry. I like that."

Wilson nodded. "But at the end of the day, it is us, the practical men, on whom the church depends. We must be vigilant! A minister, no matter how wise in the spiritual field, is apt to be imprudent when it comes to money—do you agree, Roxbury?"

"I do. Dr. Folsom may know many things; I wouldn't care to judge. But—" Eyebrows raised like a conductor's baton, Roxbury caught the attention of his friend, who nodded with him as he pronounced final judgment: "Can she read a balance sheet?"

This scenario may be a tiny bit overdrawn, but it portrays a power game that plays out subtly in more than a few congregations. Knowledge and a sense of competence about money—the ability to "read a balance sheet"—in too many congregations function to restrict financial influence to a few. This situation disenfranchises the rest, and silences some of those who, though they are not money experts, understand the congregation's mission. Financial statements should be part of the solution to this problem. The statements should inform those who know how to read them and provide an entry point for those who want to learn.

The purpose of a treasurer's report is to simplify and summarize the basic facts about an organization's finances. Its actual function in too many congregations is to intimidate new board members and stifle congregational participation in decision making. Sometimes the clergy leader manages to join the finance in-group—this can take years or decades—but just as often the mystique of money marginalizes clergy, too.

Worst of all, too many treasurers' reports distort the picture, confirming false, if sometimes comforting, notions about how the congregation gets its money and what it does with it.

No one is lying, necessarily (though with figures you can lie without half meaning to). It's simply that the treasurer's report is such a powerful document that people can't resist slanting it their way. When it comes to budgets, most governing boards are split between the haves and the have-nots, the Scrooges and the Cratchits, the green eyeshades and the rose-colored glasses. On both sides of the divide, a certain hubris prevails. The green-eyeshade people pride themselves on practicality and hard-nosed regard for facts. Meanwhile, the rose-colored-glasses party boasts of having vision, generosity, and faith in God's abundance. The treasurer's report can foster fantasies of limitless resources, or (as more often happens) it can reinforce a penny-pinching attitude that thwarts experiment and vision.

Fortunately, most board members stand between these two extremes—they feel the congregation's greater purpose deeply, but they know there is no free lunch. It is this group that needs to take charge of the treasurer's report and make it do its job. Its first job is to tell the truth, which is more difficult than it sounds. Telling the truth means giving enough detail but not too much, and accurately gauging the resources available without implying that those limits can't be changed.

Where is it written that the treasurer's report has to be the second or third item on the board agenda? Surely it was someone who wanted to make sure that the board would begin its thinking with the available resources and, like Procrustes, trim the congregation's mission to fit. A better sequence begins with discussion of the congregation's mission and goals, followed by the budget in its proper supporting role.

If the financial statements in your congregation fall short of the ideal—and they probably do—correcting the situation can be tricky. In many congregations the clergy leader initially has little or no power in the money area. In this situation one of the best ways to influence events is through asking questions. This chapter will equip you with a list of simple questions you can innocently ask after the treasurer's report is given. Ask. And ask. And ask. Ask until others start to ask as well, and until the finance mandarins find it less annoying to improve their statements than to make excuses for them.

Blessed Reassurance

Before we get to questions, though, let's look at what people usually want to know from a financial statement. The most basic concern that people have about a treasurer's report is that the records are in order and that unaccounted leakage, whether from theft or errors, is kept to a minimum. People want to be reassured so that they can relax and stop thinking about money for another month. In practice, this is the one job treasurer's reports accomplish pretty well. Many of them are so cryptic or so overwhelming that 90 out of every 100 members never try to read them, but are reassured by force of weight and heft that all is well. Of the remaining 10 people, no more than one emerges having learned much, but the other nine look to that one, just as the other 90 look to the 10, to warrant that no one is stealing anything. Everyone is reassured.

Unfortunately, their reassurance is unjustified; a treasurer's report proves no such thing. Only an independent audit, which every congregation ought to have each year, can do that. Larger congregations (with a budget over about half a million) should hire an accountant versed in the oddities of nonprofit bookkeeping to perform a formal audit every year. Smaller congregations can instead appoint an audit committee, independent of the treasurer and finance committee, to review the books, verify a random sample of transactions by comparing the bank statement with the paperwork on file, and report the result of its investigation. A few congregations have an even better idea—they team up with a neighboring congregation of about the same size and budget and trade auditing teams. This approach provides much better protection against theft or carelessness, and may yield useful suggestions for improved financial practices.

The job of the treasurer's report is to communicate. It should answer the big questions members and leaders have about the congregation's ownership and use of resources. That means the treasurer needs to produce different reports for different audiences—with computers, a much easier task these days than it once was. For in-house use, an operations statement with 114 income and expense lines helps those responsible for programs to control costs. But for the governing board, such a detailed report conceals the forest with too many trees. A one-page statement of income and expense, with enough budget comparison to show whether there are major deviations from the plan, is plenty. If there are special funds whose balances matter from month to month (for instance, a building fund while construction is under way), those can be reported separately. A simple treasurer's report helps to keep board members' attention focused on the big picture, and discourages them from taking board time asking questions about tiny items out of idle curiosity.

The annual report to the whole congregation should include a similarly uncomplicated operations statement, and also a balance sheet, showing assets and liabilities. Both statements should cover any "special" funds, so that everything of consequence is disclosed, and all that is missing is detail.

Each version of the treasurer's report should be tailored to its audience, and should address itself to the decisions that leaders and members need to make about the congregation's spending and the members' giving. Here are some questions you can ask to influence the treasurer's report in this direction.

Asking the Right Questions

Does our budget support the congregation's mission and goals? A corporate director wants to know: "Are we making a profit?" Too many congregational board members ask the same question, with a slight adjustment: "Are we breaking even?" But breaking even is not a congregation's purpose; the purpose is to change lives in ways consistent with the congregation's mission, and the budget is part of the plan for doing that.

The local paper in my town asked a new minister what new programs he planned to initiate. He said, "The church of Jesus Christ is not a new program. We're going to continue what we have been doing for 2,000 years." That's one point of view; I have a different one. I think congregations change lives by continually clarifying their mission and by periodically discerning a new vision of how to carry it out. Needs change, neighborhoods change, generations change, and the resources and talents of a congregation change, as does its membership. God may or may not change—that is a debated question—but there can be no doubt that our understanding of our calling as a congregation is always imperfect and needs to be reworked, not in every moment but every two or three years.

"Does our budget support the congregation's mission and goals?" If you ask this question regularly, sooner or later the financial folk will preempt you by highlighting this year's special goals in their statements. If a new lay ministry staff member has been added this year, his or her salary line will have an asterisk. If a new worship service has been added, the report may sprout a sidebar that shows items of expense and income related to that service, and how they compare to what was estimated. If the congregation hopes to become a more helpful force in the community, the report will emphasize how well the congregation is achieving its goal of spending money for that purpose. Often the first sign that a program is floundering is its failure to spend its budget. If the congregation really means what it says when it sets goals, some of the "exceptions" to which the financial statement should call leaders' attention are items whose spending is under budget.

Some congregations have gone so far as to turn their whole income-and-expense report inside out and make it a "program budget." Each category of expense, from heating oil to clergy salaries, is allocated to one or more of the congregation's biggest program areas. This is an interesting exercise, and I respect the impulses behind it, but I see three major problems with using it as a regular practice: First, it relies on subjective decisions about what percentage of, say, the electric bill, should be allotted to social outreach and what percentage to worship. Consequently, the report tells as much about the mind of the person who constructed it as it does about the congregation. Second, it makes it difficult for the treasurer's report to answer other essential questions, some of which you'll find below. And third, by calling attention to all of the congregation's priorities, it obscures this year's short list of top priorities and new ideas, to which the report should direct special attention. Ongoing programs are important, too, but new, revived, and enhanced program efforts require more attention.

Unexpected Expenses and Shortfall

Are we progressing as expected toward our goals, or do we need to change our plans? Many congregations treat their budget as if each line were a little bank account, filled at the beginning of the fiscal year and spent as the year goes on. Committee chairs and program leaders say, "We got $300 more this year," or "We can't do that, because our budget is almost all spent." This is understandable, and to a degree helpful, because one function of the budget is to regulate spending. If the flower committee "gets" $300, and the price of flowers rises, the budget cues them to look for ways to cut corners. The "bank account" idea also protects important but unsexy items (pension contributions, denominational assessments, janitorial supplies) by sealing each into a compartment of its own. All this helps the congregation to stay on budget.

But "staying on budget" is not the congregation's mission any more than "breaking even." The congregation's mission is to change lives. In this light, it makes more sense to think of the budget not as a set of bank accounts but as a road map. If, in the course of a trip, you find that you have deviated from the course you set at the beginning, you may or may not want to return to it. What matters is reaching the destination, not sticking to the plan.

To be a bit less metaphorical, when fuel oil prices rise, many board members' impulse is to find somewhere to cut the budget. From the bank-account perspective that makes sense. But from the point of view of ministry and mission, it will more often make sense to raise money, rather than cut program, to balance the budget.

This issue is a bit like this scenario:

> *You and your spouse are on the way to a stage play you have been looking forward to. In your pocket are two tickets, for which you paid $150 each. When you arrive, you discover you have lost the tickets on the way. There is no time to go back and look for them, and they are good only for this performance. So you have to decide: Will you buy new tickets, or just go home?*

If you ask this question in a group, you'll probably find that some people choose one answer, some the other. Here's a second scenario:

A month before the play, a pickpocket takes $300 from you. The next day you pass by the box office for the play you want to see. Do you go ahead and buy the tickets anyway?

Most people, given this version of the story, buy the tickets. Why the difference? In the first scenario, those who decide to go home without seeing the play say something like, "I've spent $300 on this play already, and now it's going to be another $300. No play is worth $600." But the same people, given the second version, might say, "The pickpocket has nothing to do with it. Losing $300 is too bad, but if I could afford the play before the loss I probably can still afford it afterward."

But from a strict financial point of view, the situations are identical. Either way, I'm out $300, and I have to decide whether to spend $300 on a play. Whether I lost the first $300 in theater tickets or in cash is irrelevant. That money is lost—sunk, as economists are wont to say. The "sunk cost fallacy"[1] is the mistake of giving too much weight to sunk costs when making new decisions. What matters is how much the play is worth to me and whether I can still afford it.

A congregation's situation is analogous when it has an unexpected expense or income shortfall. Let's say the organ needs repair. Should this mean hiring fewer soloists? Maybe—but not because the cost increase involves the organ rather than the water bill. Soloists are just as important (and as unimportant) as they were before. The question is not "How can we save money so the music doesn't cost more than we budgeted?" but "How can we achieve our mission, given the resources available?" The answer may be cutting soloists, or cutting something outside the music area, or—I admit this is my favorite—raising money from the congregation to fix the organ, so the congregation's work can go on as planned.

Giving Trends

What is the trend in people's giving to support the congregation's work? The most important resource congregations have is people's loyalty, which is expressed in many ways, none more revealing than their rate of giving.

Giving is not the only measure of a congregation's vitality, of course. In fact, it is what economists would call a "lagging indicator," registering changes somewhat later than "leading" indicators like attendance and new memberships. But generous giving represents a higher level of commitment than merely attending or even joining. So giving trends offer both an indication of the number of people and the strength of their support.

The treasurer's report needs to show both long- and short-term trends. For the short term, somewhere the treasurer's report should say how much money has flowed into the congregation this year and last, compared to a reasonable expectation. Voluntary giving varies seasonally. Many congregations have a cash-flow slump over the summer and a bulge of large gifts near the end of the tax year. One of the most common forms of treasurer-induced panic on boards is the September alarm call that member giving has "fallen behind." Behind what? Behind three-fourths of the calendar year's budget. This "problem" often is addressed by greeting members in the first fall newsletter with the announcement that something is wrong, and they should catch up on their pledge payments to correct the situation. But most of the time nothing is wrong. If someone would take the trouble to look back and see how much of the year's giving usually happens by September, it turns out that the congregation needs to be congratulated for improving.

To get long-term giving trends, someone has to go back into old records and compare present giving with that of past years. It is an interesting and revealing exercise to chart total and per-family giving over 30 years, with an adjustment for inflation. This is easy enough for anyone who knows how to use a spreadsheet.[2] Before you show the chart to your governing board, ask its members to guess in what past year people gave the most to the congregation, altogether and per family. In long-established congregations, people often hark back to the 1950s or early 1960s, which they remember, or have been told, was the golden age. In many cases, though, one or both figures will have peaked much more recently than that. Many congregations learn that their golden era, in financial terms, is now!

Questions of Compensation

How much do we pay the clergy and staff? One of the things I got used to when I became a minister was that anyone who wanted to know how much I was paid could find out. I have been surprised to learn that this is not true in every congregation. Clergy and staff salaries are lumped together, or combined with other things, so that it is possible only to guess what any individual is paid. Where this practice is followed, I'm sure people feel they have a good reason for it, but to me it looks like an extension of the wider culture's secretiveness frenzy about money. We have little hope of leading people to share their financial stories if the congregation itself is secretive about the one number—let's be honest—that even dedicated non-financial-statement readers look for: the clergy leader's salary. What people don't know they guess, and human nature being what it is, people are apt to guess that they are paying their clergy and staff more adequately than they are.

Even congregations that try to disclose salaries often bungle the job. Sometimes the value of a parsonage is simply not mentioned, creating an impression of extreme penury. More frequently the compensation is overstated. Here is the clergy salary section of a typical income-and-expense report at First Church at Flintskin Corners:

Table 5.1.
Typical financial statement

Minister	
Salary	35,000
Housing allowance	15,000
Expense allowance	2,000
Pension	7,500
Health insurance	8,000
Life insurance	150
	67,650
Staff salaries & benefits	
Education director	35,000
Music director	20,000
Youth mnister	10,000
	65,000

Nine out of 10 members, wondering (now let's be really honest) whether the minister makes more or less than they do, will look at this list and decide that he is paid $67,650. Those whose own salary is $100,000 or more will think this seems quite fair, while those who are paid less will marvel aloud that anyone can pull down such a princely sum by working only an hour a week.

But of course we know that the minister, the Rev. Rudy Valentine, makes no such amount; $67,650 is the total cost to the congregation, but that is not meaningful to most people. They are looking for a figure they can compare with other salaries, especially their own, to see whether they are comfortable with it. Most employees know what their own annual income is, but have no idea what it costs their employer to provide benefits.

There is no perfect way to tell congregants how much the clergyperson is paid. The number most nearly comparable to a normal salary is salary plus housing, $50,000 in the case of Mr. Valentine. But this number appears nowhere in the presentation! In consequence, most people look at the total that does appear, and mentally compare that to their own income.

The real story is much better told this way:

Table 5.2
Better financial statement

Salaries	
Minister	50,000
Education director	30,000
Music director	16,000
Youth minister	10,000
	106,000
Benefits	
Pension	7,500
Health insurance	8,000
Life insurance	150
	15,650

Notice that the salary and housing allowance are combined on one line. Does this practice endanger the tax treatment of the housing allowance? No—so long as the governing board adopts the housing allowance in advance of payment and records the action in the board minutes, it does not matter how the numbers are arranged in reports. Note also that the salaries of other staff are separated from benefits, making their salaries, too, comparable to those of other employees.

You may notice also that the professional expense allowance has disappeared. That's right. Professional expense reimbursements are not compensation; they are part of the congregation's cost of doing business, and should be placed in an appropriate expense category (perhaps administration or staff training and support).

If you propose restructuring the way clergy salaries are presented, someone will no doubt bring up the housing allowance itself. Laypeople generally imagine that the housing allowance makes clergy compensation much more valuable than it appears. This is a legitimate point—the value of the housing allowance increases the effective salary of clergy. As a rule, though, the effect is much smaller than most people imagine. Personally, I wish Congress would do away with special treatment for clergy; it's constitutionally doubtful, and I think it costs us more in envy than it saves in taxes.[3]

Some of us actually pay more in taxes as clergy than we would as laypeople. Here are the facts: clergy who qualify for the housing allowance are treated better than laypeople on their income tax. However, clergy have to pay a self-employment tax (SECA) of 15.3 percent in place of the social security payroll tax (FICA) of 7.65 percent paid by most employees. For most clergy, the advantage and the disadvantage roughly balance out. Of course, as usual with taxes, it is the more affluent who benefit more.

Table 5.3:
Does ordination help or hurt with taxes?

	Example 1	Example 2	Example 3
Salary	20,000	35,000	100,000
Housing Allowance	6,000	10,000	24,000
Income tax bracket	15.0%	27.5%	30.5%
Housing allowance advantage	900	2,750	7,320
Social Security disadvantage	(1,989)	(3,443)	(6,120)
Benefit of deducting half of SECA	298	947	1,867
Net advance (disadvantage)	(791)	254	3,067

Table 5.3 shows the effect of ordination on three clergypersons. All are single, and none is exempt from social security tax.[4] I've chosen reasonable levels of housing expense, given the salary, and assigned an income-tax bracket based on typical levels of deductions and exemptions. I've calculated the benefit of the housing allowance and the extra cost of self-employment tax, and added back the benefit of being able to deduct half of the self-employment tax from income tax. Note that the parson with the lowest income actually pays $791 more taxes than she would if she were not ordained. For the one with the average income of $45,000, the net benefit of ordination is $254, or pretty close to nothing. The high-income clergyperson gets a tax advantage of $3,067. If he is married to a brain surgeon, a higher tax bracket and housing cost would make the advantage even larger. Still, I believe salary plus housing is the best of the imperfect alternative ways of presenting clergy salaries, and this sum should appear in all financial statements.[5]

Serving Ourselves

How much do we give away for works of compassion, and how much do we spend on serving our own members? Some congregations have embarked on ambitious programs of charitable giving. This is a good idea from a number of perspectives. It is one of the historic functions of the Christian church to provide for the less fortunate—a role that in the Jewish community is played mostly by Jewish charities rather than by the synagogue as such. Some congregations "tithe"; others give as much as half of their revenues away. A congregation becomes more credible in asking people to be generous when it uses its own resources generously.

Unfortunately, this credibility is squandered in too many congregations by careless lumping of charitable giving with other payments. In Protestant churches it is still too common to lump all payments to national and regional denominational bodies together with "benevolences." This practice may have made sense in the 19th century when a main work of many denominations was to maintain missions, hospitals, and orphanages overseas. These days, many mainline denominations spend most of their money on offices and salaries for people whose main job is to serve and support congregations. If the benevolence section of a local congregation's budget is to regain some of its moral force, this part of the denominational assessment needs to be moved elsewhere.

Incidentally, I do not mean to suggest that congregations ought to stint on their denominational assessments. Indeed, it seems to me that the recent trend toward stinginess by congregations to their regional and national bodies is shortsighted. The relation of a congregation to its denominational organizations is analogous to that of individual members to the congregation. The congregation asks people to give generously to support its work. If at the same time it resists supporting its denomination well, it takes the risk of influencing its members by example.

Assets and Liabilities

What does the congregation own, and what does it owe? A final question worth asking until it is answered concerns the congregation's assets and liabilities. A balance sheet, like the one we made in chapter 2, answers this question well. In many congregations there are numerous special funds, given or set aside for flowers, furnishings, a memorial garden, or other purposes. Many treasurers' reports simply ignore these, as if the committees that control them were not part of the congregation. Even large endowments sometimes are essentially concealed, in part from fear that if the average member knew how much the congregation had, he or she would feel less obligation to support it. But as with other kinds of secrecy, what people know does less harm than what people imagine.

I know clergy who have accepted leadership of churches whose leaders had innocently failed to mention large debts that hampered the churches' capacity for ministry. I say "innocently," because I trust in human nature; you say what you like.

A balance sheet, including every asset and every liability, is a necessary part of a complete treasurer's report, at least annually. Land and buildings are traditionally listed at cost, which is silly enough in 30-year-old buildings. In older congregations the "cost" of the real estate may be two hundred Continental dollars, or some rifles for the local Wampanoags. A more meaningful figure would be a current appraisal of the property—though religious buildings are as hard to appraise as they sometimes are to sell. Often there is no really good solution to this problem; what is most important is to list every piece of property and state how it was valued.

If it is true, as we have often heard, that you can tell more about a person's real religion from his checkbook than from his espoused theology, the same is surely true of congregations. Even better than a checkbook is a well-drawn, honest treasurer's report. While it is rare for clergy to control financial statements personally, we can exercise the power of asking the right questions.

CHAPTER 6

Advocating for Fairness

There are wise people who talk ever so knowingly and complacently about "the working classes," and satisfy themselves that a day's hard intellectual work is very much harder than a day's hard manual toil, and is righteously entitled to much bigger pay. Why, they really think that, you know, because they know all about the one, but haven't tried the other. But I know all about both; and so far as I am concerned, there isn't money enough in the universe to hire me to swing a pickaxe thirty days, but I will do the hardest kind of intellectual work for just as near nothing as you can cipher it down—and I will be satisfied, too.

Mark Twain
A Connecticut Yankee in King Arthur's Court

Most of us who choose to enter the ministry, rabbinate, or priesthood do so with at least some sense of financial sacrifice. For a given level of effort, most members of the clergy could make more money doing something else. Service to others and to God, not the quest for money, is the heart and the root meaning of "ministry." This knowledge makes it difficult for many of us to face the fact that, even more than most people, we must speak for ourselves when it is time for our employers to decide about our pay. We also have to advocate for others on the staff. The role of advocate can and should be shared by concerned laypeople, but these lay advocates can be effective only if we make our expectations clear.

Because so many clergy are uncomfortable advocating or negotiating about salaries, they often are not only underpaid but angry about it. It would be one thing to negotiate effectively and then accept a low salary. But many clergy seem to feel that fair pay should be offered without negotiations. When it is not, low pay can lead to a downward spiral of resentment, which can make us even more tongue-tied when it comes time to talk salary.

The exact process of setting compensation varies. In congregational polities (for example, Baptist and Unitarian Universalist churches, the United Church of Christ, and synagogues), the salary decision usually flows from a personnel or similar committee to the governing board to the congregation for approval. In connectional polities, salaries are set by regional bodies— usually based on a standard scale that takes into account seniority, leadership responsibility, and the size of the congregation. The general trend in the United States, though, is for decision making about salary to gravitate toward the ultimate source of the money—almost always the members of the local congregation. If clergy leaders of congregations do not advocate for fair compensation for themselves and other staff, salaries are apt to stagnate.

The aureole of grandiose humility that is supposed to surround clergy in our culture can inhibit us from advocating for ourselves in this (or any other) arena. In 1899, Thorstein Veblen described a persistent attitude: "Few, if any members of any body of clergy . . . would avowedly seek an increase of salary for gain's sake, and if such avowal were openly made by a clergyman, it would be found obnoxious to the sense of propriety among his congregation."[1] Partly in consequence of such attitudes, mainline Protestant ministerial salaries have fallen behind those of other professions that require comparable preparation.[2] While rabbis are still relatively well paid, it would, I think, be foolish to assume that synagogues are immune from the cultural and economic trends that have depressed the salaries of other clergy.

Competition with the Mass Media

One trend that has affected clergy salaries is the growth of the mass media. A preacher nowadays has to stand up against eight or 10 broadcast alternatives. In my first church, we experimented with a hearing-assist system that used ordinary FM radio receivers. The one man willing to use it said he was the only member of the congregation who could change religions in the middle of the sermon.

Mass communication affects everyone who performs before a group for a living. Take musicians: in 1900, my great-grandfather William Guy played fiddle in the town band in Tekonsha, Michigan. The band and great-grandma Lida's musical group, the Mandolin Club, provided the finest music available to Tekonsha's 2,000 residents. In 1900 most small towns had bands and other musical ensembles; today most do not, in part because townspeople have access to recordings of better performers than a little town can muster. There is something irreplaceable about a live performance—musical or homiletic—but not everyone knows it, and even those who do know unconsciously compare live performers with the world's top performers.

The same trend that affects clergy and musicians affects all performers (comedians, politicians, athletes, newscasters, actors) and also those who "perform" more indirectly (novelists, filmmakers, inventors, computer-game designers, and comic-book artists). A few people earn millions of dollars a year in each of these occupations, while the great majority make barely enough to live on.

How can we sustain adequate clergy salaries, given the trend toward global competition? We need to identify and advertise the unique benefits of ministry up close and in person. Skill at pastoral care, and at developing small-group ministries, workplace ministries, study groups tailored to local issues and interests—these are contributions only a physically present person can make. We need to do these things and to publicize that we and the staff team we lead have done them, so as to highlight those areas in which comparison with Billy, Jimmy, Pat, and Tammy Faye work to our advantage.

At the same time, we need to accept that we are, among other things, performers, and that laypeople evaluate us as such. Since the 1960s, Protestant seminaries have periodically announced that preaching, as the center of the clergy leader's work, is passé. A study group at one major divinity school detailed its history of such pronouncements, each accompanied by a decision to teach something else instead—counseling, multimedia events, participatory worship, or video production. Each time feedback from alumni and their churches carried the same message: "We want good preachers." The school scrapped its innovative program and brought back preaching until it was again pronounced passé. We know that ministry is more than a performance, but that does not excuse us from performing well. More than ever before, the tone and mood of the whole worship experience are under close scrutiny by people whose standards and tastes are shaped by continual exposure to polished and professional performers. If clergy salaries are to keep pace, we need to hone our presentation skills.

Disappearance of Free Labor

A second trend that affects clergy and staff compensation is the decline in the supply of skilled, experienced women willing to work for little or no pay. The typical congregation in the 1950s and '60s depended heavily on such women. As volunteers they required little supervision, and as paid staff they worked for low salaries on the logic that theirs was a "second income." Some congregations have fully adjusted to the disappearance of this resource, but by no means all. If your congregation wonders why it cannot hire a religious educator for one-fourth of the starting salary of a schoolteacher, a musician for six times what it costs to contract with an organist for a wedding, or a youth minister for twice the hourly wages of a teenage baby-sitter, it would be well to wonder whether you unconsciously expect an application from Lucy Ricardo or Donna Reed. People with professional skills expect—and can command—professional compensation, and traditionally female jobs are no longer an exception. There are still willing volunteers, but they expect, much more than in years past, that their volunteer experience will be well-planned and rewarding. In contrast to the situation 30 years ago, congregations require more and better-compensated staff.

Some senior clergy fail to advocate for adequate salaries for other staff in the belief that staff and clergy are competing for a fixed pot of money. This is a losing game. Religion is competitive today. Increasing numbers of Americans, whatever they were raised to be, feel little obligation to attend a church or synagogue. Nontraditional religious options beckon from every side. In this environment, only excellence will do, and clergy cannot provide it alone. We depend more than ever on musicians, office workers, sextons, educators, volunteer coordinators, and administrators to make sure that everything we do is done well. If you need no other reason to advocate for above-average compensation for the rest of the staff, consider this: few things you can do will benefit you more.

Divergent Standards of Fairness

Our society does not have a clear standard of fairness in compensation, and actual levels vary widely among occupations. In an economy where schoolteachers average $41,000 a year, football players can make $5 million, and a few corporate CEOs make hundreds of millions, who is to say that clergy salaries, which average about $40,000, are too low, too high, or just right? And how can the variation in clergy salaries be justified? Small congregations require at least as much skill to lead as large ones, though the skills are different. Doesn't justice require equal salaries for clergy, or perhaps a standard scale based on experience? Some denominations have such scales but find it difficult to prevent wealthy or generous congregations from offering more to the candidates they want, and poor or stingy ones from offering less. It is difficult, amid the dissonance, to decide what salary is fair for a given position.

On top of all this confusion, many lay leaders do not seem to connect "fair" to "compensation" at all. Instead, salary levels function for many people mostly as a badge of status. Capitulating, at least tongue-in-cheek, to this attitude, Charles Merrill Smith, in *How to Become a Bishop without Being Religious*, one of the few really funny books ever written about churches, advised ministers in 1965 to seek finance committee members

> whose annual income exceeds substantially the most optimistic estimate of what the church might pay its pastor in a period of unprecedented economic health. This is because it is unreasonable to expect anyone to vote the pastor more money than he makes himself. It puts too great a strain on human nature.[3]

Many governing board members express their low opinion of religious work by asking, when a staff or clergy position comes open, "What is the least we have to pay to get the job done?" This is puzzling to us clergy, who are trained to think of compensation in terms of fairness, rather than competition. To feel confident in advocating for ourselves and those who work with us, it is important to develop a well-grounded philosophy of what compensation is "fair."

Our society lacks an accepted standard of fair pay. It is therefore difficult to discuss pay in a congregation's board or personnel committee, composed of people who work in diverse settings, retired people, and people who do not work for pay at all. Because their assumptions are largely unconscious, people debating salary levels may assume they disagree in their evaluation of a staff person when their differences are actually philosophical. In this as in so many other areas of congregational life, clergy must understand the various assumptions people bring to the conversation and try to help people to communicate about them. The most influential theories fall into three main families: the labor theory of value, the theory of intrinsic value, and market theory.

Labor Theory of Value

The "labor theory of value" holds that the value of a good or service consists in the amount of labor that has been invested in it. A handmade doorknob, for example, sells for more than the rough brass casting it was made from, because of the time several machinists—operating a lathe, a drill press, and a polishing machine—have invested in it. Added to the total is some share of the time that went into making the machine tools, building the factory, delivering the product, and so on, and you get the fair value of the finished doorknob.

Implicit in the labor theory is a basic equality of value among workers. It follows that a worker's pay should be related to the amount of work he or she does, more than to the nature of the work. Few people hold this theory consciously or absolutely, but it pops up nonetheless. Many small congregations, for example, have a hard time breaking free of the idea that Mary in the office and Fred on the organ bench and Wilhelmina in the Sunday school should all be paid at the same hourly rate. Having started them out at the same pay level, it's hard to give a larger raise to one than to the others.

One way to justify pay differences within the labor theory is to accept that people should be compensated not only for the hours they spend on the job, but also for those spent in preparation. For example, an educator can make more per hour than a secretary, because of the additional schooling the job requires. The educator must be paid for working today, and also for time spent in college. Of course, it is complicated, using this kind of reasoning, to arrive at precise salary numbers.

Still, the labor theory of value has continuing appeal. Minimum-wage laws express the idea that an hour's work has, if not an equal value for all workers, at least a common base value that employers ought to honor. In religious communities we would like to affirm that every human being equally bears the divine image. When board members say, "But aren't we supposed to be an exemplary employer?" often they mean the congregation ought to treat its employees more equitably. So the labor theory persists, at least to the extent that differences in hourly compensation need to be explained and justified.

Intrinsic Value

A second theory of fair compensation begins with the idea that wages should reflect the intrinsic value of the work, including both its difficulty and the importance of the goods or services produced. This theory is embodied in the concept of "comparable worth" used in lawsuits and legislation designed to equalize the pay for jobs traditionally performed by women with the pay for jobs traditionally held by men. In many companies, for instance, secretaries, whose work requires a high school diploma, typing and computer skills, and considerable social tact, have been paid less than janitors. This arrangement technically gives "equal pay for equal work," because all secretaries—female and male—are paid the same, and all janitors—male and female—are paid the same.

One possible solution is to reduce the underlying stereotypes about "women's work" and "men's work" by recruiting more men to be secretaries and more women to be janitors, but this method is slow and uncertain. The comparable-worth approach requires detailed studies of job qualifications and the work to be done, so that each job can be ranked by its intrinsic value and jobs with equal value are paid equally. The employer then defends any sex-discrimination lawsuit by explaining any difference in wages by the rankings of the jobs. Comparable worth is cumbersome, but has no doubt succeeded at correcting some traditional male-female wage discrepancies more quickly than they would have been corrected otherwise.

However you may feel about this kind of social engineering, the intrinsic-value theory underlying it has some appeal. It offends our sense of justice when price and intrinsic value get too seriously out of sync, as when an elementary school teacher in an inner-city neighborhood can barely pay the rent, while a rap star who flunked out of the same school makes millions spouting sexist garbage. The importance of the teacher's service is, we feel, quite high, while that of the rap star may be less than zero. Pay should be related to the underlying value of the work.

Congregations are, needless to say, hardly immune from sex-based job stereotypes. Historically secretaries, educators, and musicians, and more recently assistant and associate clergy, have often have women, and their pay has been relatively low. When my mother started as a church musician in 1953, no one doubted that her compensation should take into account the fact that hers was a "second income." As I write, she is preparing the church for the "sticker shock" they will experience when she retires and they try to hire a younger musician with comparable skills. It is a transition many congregations will need to face if they are going to succeed in a new century.

Market Theory

The third major theory that drives discussion about salaries in congregations takes a fundamentally different tack. Market theory treats labor as a marketplace commodity. It assumes that employers try to pay the least they can for a given kind and quality of work, and employees try to get the most they can. If both workers and employers are free to choose alternatives (an especially troublesome assumption in the labor market), they will arrive at a "price" for labor that is economically efficient.

Market prices, including pay rates, are determined by the "law of supply and demand." For every good or service there is a relationship between the price and the amount the public will buy. This relationship is called the demand curve. There is also a relationship, called the supply curve, between the price and the amount producers will produce. This relationship will be familiar to those who took an economics course; the demand and supply curves for diamonds look something like this:

Figure 6.1
Demand and Supply Curves: Diamonds

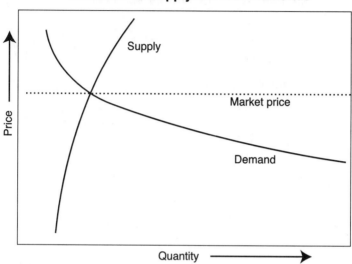

If the price of an item is low, people will want more of it than if the price is high. The reverse is true of supply: if the price is high, producers will produce more than they would if it were lower. The crossover point, where supply equals demand, is the price actually found in the marketplace.

We have already noted that in the real world, price (including the price of labor) does not always match intrinsic value, and market theory explains why. Compare the price of diamonds with the price of drinking water. Diamonds have some practical use in industry, but for the most part they are luxuries—ornaments and status symbols. Clean water is a necessity of life, without which we die quickly. There can be no question that water's value, from a human point of view, is much higher. But the price of diamonds (by weight or by volume) is many times the price of water. Why?

Diamonds, as we saw in figure 6.1, have a supply curve that is steep and far to the left. In other words, no matter how high the price, diamond companies do not increase production very much, partly because diamonds are scarce and hard to mine, and partly because the diamond industry is tightly controlled by the DeBeers cartel, which limits production.

Water, by comparison, is much more plentiful than diamonds, so its supply curve is low and flat. In addition, the water industry is heavily regulated to ensure that communities have the water they need.

Figure 6.2

Demand and Supply Curves: Water

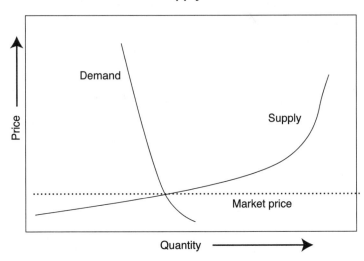

If prices increase, sellers can increase the supply of water (up to a point, anyway) quite easily. The fact that people would pay anything they had to for a small supply of water (see how steep the demand curve is) doesn't matter, because the two curves cross at a low price.

According to market theory, the pay rate for a job depends on the shape and position of the demand and supply curves for that job. The number of hours involved and the intrinsic value of the work both affect pay levels—but they do so by reshaping the supply and demand curves. As a description of what actually happens, there is nothing especially controversial about this theory. Labor unions tacitly endorse it when they go on strike—artificially restricting the supply of labor—to raise wages (wages are, of course, the "price" of labor). Professions, including the clergy, impose educational requirements and other limits on the number of competing claimants for a job. They do this to ensure quality, but a welcome side effect, from the professionals' point of view, is to reduce competition for positions, making the supply curve steeper and causing salaries to rise. Periodically congregations have resisted such requirements, insisting that what matters in a clergyperson is not formal education but less tangible (not to mention cheaper) qualities like inspiration, vocation, and charisma.

Market theory does not explain all economic behavior equally well.

Once in a while people pay more for something than they have to—I remember, for example, paying a Navajo vendor the six dollars he asked for a piece of turquoise jewelry, though it was clear he expected me to bargain. But I didn't feel like bargaining with someone to whom six dollars clearly meant more than it meant to me. Suppliers, too, sometimes persist in producing something buyers won't buy. The classic example is the devoted manufacturer of buggy whips. My great-grandfather Guy, the fiddle player, owned a shop where he sold horse tackle, including buggy whips; his wife, Lida, was a milliner. Their timing was unfortunate: in 1910 or so, demand for buggy whips and ladies' hats dried up. They kept on supplying, but consumers stopped demanding, and they both went out of business. Congregations risk the same result when they continue to serve up 40-year-old versions of the faith. But thanks to endowments, tax exemptions, and other bulwarks against market forces, congregations are much slower to go broke, even when it might be better if they did.

The market concept describes economic behavior remarkably well—even the behavior of clergy. I spent seven years observing the job market for Unitarian Universalist ministers, and I can testify that clergy do give weight to many factors other than salary in hunting for a position. The congregation's spiritual depth, enthusiasm, and sense of mission figure large, as do location, location, and location. Consistently, though, when a minister judged two congregations to be substantially equal in all of the intangibles, he or she invariably chose one that paid more over another that paid less. Even with clergy, money talks.

Market theory becomes controversial when people convert it from a description of what happens (an "is") to a prescription of what should happen (an "ought")—which, of course, many people do. In setting clergy and staff salaries, some board members act as though it would be positively immoral to pay more, or to offer better benefits, than the church or temple down the street. In so doing, they take the "law" of supply and demand to be not simply a description of reality, but a moral imperative.

But supply and demand are the effect, not the cause, of human values. People will buy diamonds at almost any price (or so it seemed to me when I shopped recently for an engagement present). Diamonds' flat demand curve has little to do with the objective properties of diamonds, and much to do with the mystique about them that our culture, with help from the DeBeers monopoly, has built up over the years. As clergy, we know that what congregations offer is of intrinsic value. But that value translates to fair compensation only when we advocate for it effectively.

CHAPTER 7

Advocating for Generosity

And it came to pass that the time of the year was upon them when the call went forth from the Great Temple for pledges of support for another twelvemonth. And one there was who rebuked the solicitor gruffly, saying, "Get thee hence, and return not. Verily, the Great Temple seeketh money from everlasting to everlasting." The solicitor accepted the rebuff, and said unto him quietly, "My son, when he was a child, was very costly. He was forever hungry, and was fed; he was forever wearing out or outgrowing his raiment and was clothed anew. As he increased in the stature of manhood, ever more money had I need to spend upon him. And it came to pass that the Angel of Death smote him, and he died. And lo! Now he costeth me not a cent!" And he who had rebuked him was filled with compassion and understanding, and he said, "Verily, verily, thou hast opened mine eyes; for now I see that only a dead Temple needeth no money: a live Temple needeth ever more!" And he offered up his pledge, . . . a sadder but wiser man.

Clinton Lee Scott
20th-century Universalist leader

A great deal of creative thinking goes into *not* asking people to give money to their congregations. Stewardship sermons urge people with great emphasis to give the congregation "time and talent," but ask them only indistinctly, if at all, to give money. Stewardship campaigns involve musical productions, banquets, speeches, balloons, loaves of bread, and colorful thermometers, all without direct appeals to people to give money. This curious omission is especially typical of relatively liberal "mainline" Protestant denominations, but as the American religious melting pot does its homogenizing work, it happens in a growing number of evangelical and Jewish congregations, too.

Most such congregations would be surprised to learn that they don't ask people to give money. They think they do; I think they don't. It would take a video recorder and a confrontation to convince them. The following statements, in my opinion, don't count:

- "Everything belongs to God; give some of it back."
- "Stewardship is about time, talent, and treasure."
- "Our expenses have gone up, so we need to raise 10 percent more this year if possible."
- "Our average pledge is $1,100, and we'd like to raise that to $1,200 next year. Please do your share."

None of these statements asks any particular member for any particular amount of money. Even saying "The Bible commands Christians to tithe, and as your minister, I have tithed for years," gives a curious mixed message. The minister is setting an example, but is anybody following?

Sometimes the clergy leader or one or two laypeople have learned some fund-raising techniques from their work with another congregation or a charity. They know the most important reason people give is that someone asks them to. They know that the most effective method is to ask, in person, for a particular amount of money to support a clear, exciting vision of the future. Following these principles, they may even achieve an incremental rise in giving. But it is difficult to sustain meaningful growth in giving if the institution as a whole is working against you. No one can get a congregation energized about a vision if leaders are not energized, or if they have not developed a track record of advancing the congregation's mission year after year. It is ineffective to ask people to increase their giving if the leaders are not committed, personally, to do what they are asking others to do. Volunteers who are asked to lead fund-raising efforts in this no-win situation have a short half-life.

Many congregations, asked to rank the clergy leader's main responsibilities, list "fund raising" dead last—below even "administration." Those congregations are mistaken. Because the congregation's ultimate purpose is religious, fund raising[1] (like administration) cannot prosper in the long term without active support from you as a clergy leader. The kind of support that is necessary requires few skills you do not already possess. It does require some information about the basics of effective fund raising for a congregation, so that you can make good use of skilled lay volunteers and fund-raising consultants. This chapter will explain what you need to know to give the leadership that only you can give. We will begin with some background information and historical perspective on the funding of American religion.

The Current Situation

We tend to assume that American congregations are supported strictly by the current voluntary gifts of participants. Certainly this is the source of most of their income—perhaps, for Protestant churches, as much as 90 percent,[2] but the reality is varied.

Most synagogues charge their member families dues, sometimes on a sliding scale by income. While synagogue dues are treated as a charitable contribution by the IRS, in Jewish parlance they are usually distinguished from "contributions," which begin after the basic dues are paid, and from *tzedakah*, or true charity, which does not go to the synagogue at all.[3]

In addition to the gifts of current members, most congregations rely on various kinds of endowments. The most obvious of these are held as stock portfolios that generate an annual cash income. The most common, though, are held as land and buildings, which support the congregation by providing rent-free housing for its work. Some congregations produce cash by renting space to other organizations or businesses.

Many congregations have moved toward a fee-for-service model, with much of the revenue generated by workshops, classes, concerts, bookstore sales, and similar transactions. Religious bodies recently introduced to the United States from elsewhere (for instance, Buddhist centers, Hindu temples, and mosques) tend to rely on fees for their basic income, with voluntary gift campaigns reserved for buildings and other special projects.

Subsidiary operations like schools, hospitals, and social agencies depend on a combination of fees, foundation grants, charitable gifts, and government subsidies. Politicians periodically propose to lower the constitutional barrier that now limits the use of public funds for agencies controlled by religious institutions.

Because congregations do not have to file tax returns, it is not easy to be sure how much of their income is produced in each of these ways. But while current giving is undoubtedly the largest source of funds for congregations, it is clearly not the only one or even the main one for every congregation.

Recent research has taught us something about the recent history of the support of congregations by their members. Most notably, a project led by sociologist Dean R. Hoge documents the trends and current situation of 625 churches in five denominations.[4] While the research is limited to Christian churches, it suggests some principles of broader application. Here are some points that strike me as important:

- Giving to mainline Protestant churches rose dramatically (in constant dollars) from the Depression until about 1980, and has since then declined relative to personal incomes. Some, but not all, of the money shifted to evangelical congregations.
- Rates of giving vary dramatically by denomination. Members of the Church of Jesus Christ of Latter-day Saints (Mormon) and the Assemblies of God give most, followed by evangelical Christians, mainline Protestants, and finally Roman Catholics. Protestants give about twice as much per member as Roman Catholics. Similar contrasts apply to the percentage of family income contributed.
- Since about 1950, mainline congregations have kept a growing proportion of their income for themselves and sent less to denominational headquarters. Dissatisfaction and declining trust may play a role, but higher local staff costs may be a more important cause.
- Within a typical church, families with higher incomes give more money, but the percentage of income given falls as income rises.
- The distribution of gifts is "skewed," with about 75 percent of the money coming from about 20 percent of the families. Giving is most sharply skewed in congregations where giving is highest: the difference in giving between conservative and liberal Protestants is almost entirely concentrated in the top 20 percent. These patterns are similar to those found in nonreligious charitable giving.
- Frequency of worship attendance predicts individual giving better than any other factor measured. Other important variables are age (oldest members give most) and personal religious devotion (frequent prayer, self-reported "strength" of faith, frequent Scripture reading), and time

spent participating in the congregation. Orthodox belief (e.g., biblical literalism, lack of doubt) correlates with giving, but more weakly.

- Small congregations receive larger gifts, on average, than large ones. Churches with large rental and endowment income tend to have low member contributions, and individuals who think they are less wealthy than others in the congregation give less.
- Congregations that ask for annual pledges get more money than those that request contributions on an unplanned, weekly basis. Beyond that, there is little conclusive evidence on the effectiveness of various approaches to fund raising.

This picture can be discouraging, especially to mainline Protestants. Clearly, the winners in the race for the religious dollar are churches like the Mormons and Assemblies of God, which have strict standards for giving and achieve high levels of compliance. Less-strict evangelicals do less well; mainline Protestants and Catholics (whose traditional stewardship approach has not sought strong support from middle-income members) worst of all. But it is not obvious that the typical northern Presbyterian, German Lutheran, or New England congregational church (much less a synagogue) could emulate the strict, prescriptive approach even if it chose to. It would be hard to square such an approach with the wide latitude in individual belief and historical-critical approach to the Bible that are characteristic of such churches. It is hard to argue with the Episcopal vestry member who, when his rector advocated tithing as a biblical precept, said, "So, when it comes to stewardship, we're fundamentalists?" Each congregation needs to raise money in ways compatible with its history and present character.

Variety in the Past

In defense of our favored style of fund raising, we clergy often assert the authority of tradition. But the situation of contemporary American congregations is profoundly different from that of the Hebrews in ancient Judah, the early church in Corinth, or the congregations of Europe or pre-Revolutionary America. Consequently, historical precedents are not easy to apply.

The dependence of American congregations on voluntary gifts is exceptional in the history of religious institutions. In ancient times, religion was, like law and language, an undivided aspect of a person's ethnic identity—there was no distinction between an Egyptian and a worshiper of Ra, or between a Israelite and a Jew. Accordingly, while Israel was in the wilderness, Moses imposed a "ransom" of a half-shekel per male person for the building of a sanctuary. Later, Moses asked "whoever is of a generous heart" to bring gifts of precious materials for the sanctuary, and for "All who are skillful among you" to help with construction. As various Jewish observers have pointed out, these two modes of support—an equal share for everyone, to indicate the full participation of each, and voluntary giving based on generosity and ability—reflect the persistent tension between the principle of equality and the fact of unequal ability and motivation.[5] They also illustrate the tension between voluntary contributions and fixed assessments, which has been a theme in congregational finance ever since.

In the Middle Ages, Christian churches normally depended on land granted them by the sovereign. Like the feudal estates of other noblemen, a bishop's lands were worked by serfs, who paid the bishop rents with which he supported his own household, the local churches and clergy, and the monasteries, shrines, and other Christian institutions in his bailiwick. Various side enterprises, including the sale of relics and indulgences, provided extra income to the church. Some donations were given, often by patrons who expected substantial control in exchange, but these were secondary as a source of revenue.

The sale of indulgences was, of course, one of the excesses that prompted Martin Luther in 1517 to launch the Protestant Reformation. Luther criticized the sale of indulgences on theological grounds, but he did not object to the feudal lands that were the main source of church income. It was not until the revolutions of 1789–1871, which largely dispossessed the church in France and Germany, that its funding shifted from rents to taxes. Having stripped the church (along with the rest of the nobility) of its lands, the revolutionary governments found themselves holding the responsibility for supporting Christianity if it was to be supported at all. These taxes came largely from the growth sector of the economy, the business activities of the rising middle class.[6]

Synagogues and sectarian churches, being outside the official establishment, had to look to their members for gifts. But by the nature of life on the margins of society, they served cohesive communities whose internal leadership had considerable authority. Financial assessments by a group of persecuted Anabaptists or the leaders of a medieval Jewish community cannot be called voluntary in the modern sense.

The first churches in North America were supported in a variety of ways. In the Puritan communities of New England and the Anglican strongholds of the South, the church and clergy were regarded as an essential part of the public order. Accordingly, church support came from taxes, and clergy were often provided with land as well, which they could work themselves or rent to others. During the 18th century, however, growing religious diversity made church taxes less acceptable. In Massachusetts, the last holdout, congregational churches were disestablished only in 1836, by which time the church tax was riddled with exemptions and exceptions.

With neither a state nor extensive lands to support them, American churches tried pew rents for a time, but in the end became almost entirely dependent upon voluntary gifts. Those accustomed to tax support accepted the new situation with varying degrees of grace. Meanwhile, immigrant groups and westward pioneers founded synagogues and churches that had never known another way. It was in this new situation that, in the late 19th century, Protestant denominational leaders defined and popularized a fund-raising approach they called "stewardship."[7] While rooted in a certain reading of the Bible, stewardship was an effort to raise money in a radically new situation.

Since then, the "disestablishment" of Christianity has continued. Just as in the 19th century the church had to learn how to do without taxes, religious institutions in the 21st century will need to fund themselves without the Eisenhower-era belief that support of organized religion is an indispensable requirement of middle-class respectability. Like earlier transitions, this one will require new skills and understandings of the clergy, and the unlearning of some stubborn habits.

Getting Used to "Skew"

One habit that is among the biggest barriers to effective fund raising in many congregations is resistance to the fact that relatively few people give most of the money. This imbalance is what mathematicians call "skewness." Sometimes the proportion is described in terms of the Pareto Principle, or 80-20 rule, which predicts that 80 percent of the money will given by 20 percent of the people. (Italian economist Vilfredo Pareto, writing in about 1900, formulated the hypothesis.) Money is not the only aspect of church life that is skewed. Time, loyalty, creativity, skill, and virtually every other "input" to a congregation's life is skewed: some people give much more than others. The Pareto Principle, like Murphy's Law, expresses resignation: if skewness is a law of nature, we should learn to love it, or at least get used to it.

In the Protestant churches I have worked with, capital campaigns come close to Pareto's 80-20 breakdown, but annual giving is less skewed, sometimes as low as 60-20 (20 percent of the people give 60 percent of the money). In general, the more money you raise, the more skewed the distribution. So while it may be that the low-giving freeloaders are the problem, the most promising solution almost always is to ask your largest givers to give even more. Most of the potential for new money lies in the deepest and most committed pockets, so as giving grows, the increase tends to skew the distribution even more.

What is true within a congregation seems to be true between denominations also. Denominations whose members give more money to their churches have a more strongly skewed distribution of giving. As already noted, the difference in giving between mainline and more conservative Protestant congregations is confined almost entirely to the top 20 percent of givers. Strict demands apparently produce their effect mostly among the few.

Skewness gives rise to a great deal of angst in congregations. Stewardship or canvass committees worry a great deal about the smallest givers, feeling that if only those who give under $100 a year could be persuaded to be more responsible, that would not only ease the congregation's finances; it would raise a lot more money. This is demonstrably false; the smallest givers are almost never the most productive source of increased giving. But I think that the point being expressed is really that skewed giving seems unfair.

I'm not sure I agree. If you assume that support of a congregation is a shared obligation like a working lunch, then it would make sense to share it equally. You would create, as Moses did, a system of flat taxes. But if you assume, as most Americans do, that religious participation is voluntary, then you would expect people in a congregation to vary in their interest and commitment. In other words, you would expect the distribution of commitment within a congregation to be skewed.

The ability to give is skewed as well. Income and wealth are much more strongly skewed than most people think, even in seemingly homogeneous congregations. It is a common experience in a capital campaign to discover that someone unexpectedly turns out to be able to give $100,000 or more. In the U.S. population, 56 percent of the income is received by 20 percent of the households, and 83 percent of the wealth is held by 20 percent of the households. Incomes in a typical congregation are probably less skewed than that (perhaps 40-20), but ability to give is more skewed than income. A family of four with an income of $20,000 cannot give much at all, certainly much less than a tenth of what a single person with a $200,000 income could give. When we consider the skewed distribution of ability to give, and take for granted a skewed distribution of interest and commitment, it is not surprising that giving comes out skewed. Indeed, the larger and more successful the campaign, the more skewed the giving is. The 1987 Jewish Federation campaigns received 60 percent of their money from just 1.6 percent of the givers![8]

Complaining about skewness is counterproductive. I once consulted with a congregation in a resort area whose year-round residents groused that they gave most of the money while many "summer people" gave only $25 to $100 a year. I suggested that they might want to make it a goal to succeed even better at attracting $100 gifts from summer worshipers. They initiated a direct-mail "Friends" campaign that soon generated $10,000 a year. As a result of all the new small gifts, their giving distribution is more skewed than ever!

One of the single most costly mistakes congregations make in raising money is to give too little time, attention, recognition, and priority to the top 20 percent of potential donors. In most congregations, this group gives at least three-fifths of the money, and represents perhaps 80 to 90 percent of the potential for increased giving. Fear of "elitism" often spares those with the greatest resources from carrying their fair share of the cost, and denies those with the greatest commitment the opportunity to express their faith through giving. Hospitals, universities, and symphony orchestras court wealthy people constantly. With permission and encouragement from clergy leaders, congregations can and should do likewise.

Getting Used to Pluralism

Just as levels of giving vary, so do motivations. But some congregations authorize only one motive for giving, saying for example, "We give from our awareness that everything comes from God," or "We appeal to the giver's need to give." A one-pronged strategy may work for strict, homogeneous congregations, but the rest of us need to appeal to a variety of motives, because no matter how successful we are at promoting our favored way of thinking, there will always be potential donors who have not yet come to appreciate the correctness of the official view. Here are some of the varieties of givers I have noticed:

Social Givers

One group, often including many lay leaders, seems to support the congregation mostly from the excitement of belonging to a team accomplishing a worthwhile project. Social givers respond to one another's leadership, especially leadership by example. Their giving is, at least in part, an act of reciprocity—one donor sometimes supports another's cause even when he or she has little personal interest in it. It is with this group, mainly, that the techniques of the professional fund-raisers, myself included, work best. Social givers want the "case" for a fund drive to be well prepared, and are best asked to give by someone who has given in the prospective giver's likely "bracket."

Spiritual Givers

Another group, usually smaller, including often but not always clergy, speaks of generous giving in spiritual terms. A spiritual person, these givers say, gives in response to God's generosity. This attitude has led to a surprise revival of the tithe in some liberal denominations. Spiritual givers sometimes seem almost indifferent to the specifics of the project or institution they are giving to, and this makes sense: if giving is mostly a response of gratitude to God, it is not necessary to quibble about how the money will be used. These are the sort of people who give to the panhandler on the street, not because they think it will help the panhandler, but because they think it is what Jesus (for example) would have done. In a fund drive, spiritual givers seem almost offended by much talk about the budget or the building plan. Nor does it seem to help to match them with a canvasser in their own "bracket." A spiritual giver is most likely to be influenced to grow in giving by another spiritual giver.

Dues Payers

Those in a third group think about their gifts mostly as dues or fees for service. Dues payers want to know the minimum gift they need to give to avoid being regarded as freeloaders. They are different from another group who are quite happy to freeload, but they also differ from the groups described above, for whom giving is positive in itself. Dues payers give to erase a debt created by participating in the congregation and using its services. Most synagogues show respect for this mindset by funding basic operations through membership dues. Some contemporary churches, especially those of the New Age persuasion, raise a good part of their revenue through retail sales and fees for seminars and concerts. However it structures its appeal, though, every congregation has some members who expect to be charged for what they use. In asking dues payers for support, it is important not to minimize the value of services they use. Like most people, dues payers value what they pay for; they will get more out of the congregation if they bear a substantial portion of its costs.

These three types—social givers, spiritual givers, and dues payers—do not constitute a full typology of givers.[9] Within each type are extremes: some social givers give not just to participate in a group project but to dominate the group or aggrandize themselves. Spiritual givers range from a few near-monastics who give to impoverish themselves to multitudes who give in the belief that God will shower them with reciprocal "abundance." Dues payers include the families who show up and pay only for their own weddings and funerals, as well as those who are quite willing to shoulder a full share of the "overhead costs" incidental to the services they use.

Overlying the whole range of giving styles is the continuing shift of generations. The GI generation, whose gifts and bequests will be important to American congregations for many years to come, has by now largely handed over leadership of congregations to the baby boomers, whose record of religious participation and support is so far much less consistent. The GIs believe in stable congregations, buildings, permanence, and reputation, and have been willing to make sacrifices to achieve these things. The boomers, as a group, look to religion to provide personal experiences of depth and meaning for themselves and for their children, and it is not clear to all of them that congregations have a role to play in their lives. It is obvious that all these groups—and the genX, millennial, and unnamed generations yet to follow—will think differently about their money: earning, spending, saving, and donating.

Making the Vision Clear

Because of the diversity of givers, one of the most challenging and critical aspects of successful fund raising is articulating the "case," or institutional vision, for giving. The vision statement that is most effective speaks to both head and heart, and to the many styles and generations of givers. Clergy have a central role to play in clarifying and articulating a vision that will inspire generous giving to the congregation.

A clear, concrete vision is critical for fund raising success. This is why congregations easily raise money to build buildings—an architect's model in the foyer helps all to see what their money will accomplish. The annual pledge drive is more inchoate and therefore more challenging. In most congregations, the case for annual giving is quite pale: Costs have gone up. We'd like an associate pastor. It would be nice to give the staff a raise. We wish we could afford more for world service.

Ideally, a congregation's vision would arise from a thorough planning process with wide congregational participation, but that will not always happen. What is indispensable is that the governing board, each time it asks for money, choose a central goal or goals to highlight. A vision to inspire generous giving needs to have several characteristics:

It must be concrete. Lyle Schaller, prominent author and consultant on congregational life, tells the story of a minister whose congregation had grown jaded toward the regular appeals for mission giving. So one year he borrowed a large tractor from a dealer and parked it in front of the main entrance to the church. As people walked around it to enter the narthex, he said nothing. Finally someone asked why it was there, and he announced, "That is the tractor we are going to buy and send to our farm program in Senegal." With no more fund-raising effort, the money was in hand within a week. People respond more generously to objects, pictures, and specifics than to abstractions. Make it concrete.

It must show how people will be helped. The quintessential up-to-date religious charity, in my mind, is Habitat for Humanity. It is aswim with volunteers, and it raises substantial money from congregations not known for their generosity. I'm sure its reasons for success are many, but the one that stands out for me is the fact that the beneficiaries of each Habitat project are specific people who will benefit in a clear-cut way. The lesson? Don't talk about Jewish education—trot out one of your recent bar or bat mitzvoth to give a testimonial. Don't just add an associate pastor—talk about the shut-ins who will benefit from visitation and new programs. Show how people will be helped.

It must have top leadership commitment. Nothing is more damaging than to announce a vision and a goal, then fail to realize it. This is why leaving vision to the budget or canvass committee is a mistake. The governing board and leading staff need to do more than passively endorse the vision; they must intend to achieve it, one way or another. A wan, "if we raise the money" kind of appeal risks a wan, "show us some results, and then we'll think about it" kind of response. An effective vision is one the leaders believe is realistic, that they are committed to support with their own increased giving, and that they mean to realize.

It must be articulated over and over again. Here, more than anywhere else, is where you, the clergy leader, come in. One of the unfortunate traits of "learned clergy" is that we sometimes think we have to be original. But leadership demands that we repeat ourselves. It takes about six weeks of broadcasting on all channels—oral announcements, newsletter articles, group discussions, mailings, and brochures—for a message to have sufficient penetration to affect people's behavior. It takes multiple messengers, all giving the same message. That's why it makes sense to write a "case statement" for each fund drive, so that everyone writing, speaking, or soliciting for the campaign is making the same case.

You may now be shaking your head, wondering how it is possible to lead your congregation from its current, hand-to-mouth mode of financing itself to something more visionary. This is not a simple question or an easy challenge. The first and indispensable requirement, though, is that the clergy leader must be committed to the change. By paying attention to fund-raising fundamentals year after year, you can make a difference.

Asking for Money

After establishing the vision, the next hurdle that the fund-raising committee and governing board need to face is deciding how much money to ask for. The "ask" (I apologize for this noun, a bit of fund-raising jargon; it means an agreed-upon amount to ask someone to give—if you can come up with a less awkward term I would be glad to hear from you!) takes two forms: the general ask, which is announced to the congregation as a whole, and the ask for each individual or household. It is important to make the general "ask" clear, and there is no way to do that without numbers. Here are some examples of clear general asks:

- We are asking each family to consider pledging $200 a month, or increasing last year's pledge by $10 a month.
- Please consider pledging at least $5,000 to extend our day-school building.
- Please choose the level in the following list that reflects your resources and commitment. To reach our goal, we need at least:
    - 4 gifts of $50,000 or more
    - 5 gifts of $30,000–$50,000
    - 8 gifts of $20,000–$30,000
    - 12 gifts of $10,000–$20,000
    - 100 gifts of $4,500–$10,000

The general ask needs to be specific enough that prospects and canvassers will both know whether the answer was yes or no.

After you choose an "ask," someone is sure to object that it is too high or too low for some people. That's true. But the general ask is not a demand or a prescription. Whenever it is mentioned publicly, it should be balanced by such words as these: "We know there are some in the congregation for whom this will not be possible, and others who will be able to give much more." Never mention the poor without mentioning the rich at the same time!

The general ask needs to be supplemented by a plan for asking for specific amounts from at least the top 20 percent, not of last year givers but of this year's prospects. For at least this group it is worth the time and effort to evaluate and choose an amount to ask each of them to give. If you gather a group of lay leaders, including if possible one or two bankers or financial consultants—not, of course, to reveal confidential information, but for their real-world knowledge of personal finance—you will be surprised what well-educated guesses they can produce about people's capacity and willingness to give.

Some congregations are uncomfortable with evaluation sessions and specific asks. It is a method that can backfire if it is done in a prescriptive or uncaring way. Remember, though, that you are not telling people how much they ought to give; you are deciding how much you ought to ask them for. Canvassers should be discouraged from taking a moralistic or directive tone—or worse yet, opening with, "The committee has you down for . . ." At the same time, they need to know that the number-one cause of disappointing fund-raising outcomes is canvassers who don't ask prospects for money. Canvassers need to be encouraged to ask clearly and earnestly for a specific amount. When I train canvassers, I suggest this wording, which has always made it easier for me to ask for money: "Would you consider a pledge of $___?"

In addition to specificity, there are two more tests that both the general and specific asks must satisfy. One is that the governing board, fund-raising committee, clergy, and other important leaders of the congregation commit personally to say yes to the general ask, or to their specific ask if it is less or more. It is damaging to publish a chart or rule that calls for giving far more than the leaders of the congregation actually give. It is better to ask for less, and be able to say, "Your clergy, board, and finance leaders overwhelmingly have already said 'yes' to this request."

In my experience, if you can say this, half of the members who are asked in person will say yes. (I have been saying this for a long time, and once made the mistake of saying it in a university town where I was consulting with a congregation. A professor noted my prediction, and after the campaign confronted me in front of others. "Dan," he said, "I have been keeping track, and you should know that the percentage actually was 48.6." This was the high point of my calling as a prophet.)

The other test an ask must pass is this: If half of the people we ask say yes, will we be able to accomplish the vision? This seems obvious, but it is often missed.

Traditionally, the "best" way to do a fund drive was by organizing canvassers to visit everyone at home. Many people nowadays are uncomfortable visiting or being visited at home, and I see no reason why people cannot be asked for money as effectively in a coffee shop, at work, or in a church or synagogue. No doubt a one-on-one or one-on-two visit is ideal, but as a practical matter it may make sense to reserve the most labor-intensive forms of solicitation for the top 20 percent of prospects. Getting well-prepared canvassers to that core group will repay the effort richly, and the rest can be asked for money in other ways. If you let others who would like a personal visit ask for one, it will reduce the sense of inequality, and you can be sure that those requested visits will be among the most gratifying for the canvasser. In decreasing order of effectiveness, some alternate ways of asking for gifts include small groups, larger gatherings, telephone calls, and letters. If you have clarified the vision well and publicized the "ask" effectively, those methods, too, will be successful.

In many congregations, fund raising is a closely protected preserve of a few lay leaders, which is too bad. Fund raising is asking for money, but it is not really a financial function. It is an invitation to the whole congregation to join in its vision. Giving money to support the congregation is one of the core ways people commit to a community of faith, so it is of vital concern to clergy. We can enhance the health of congregations by supporting them financially, by asking others to join us, and by helping the lay leaders to keep their focus on the fundamentals of successful fund raising: a clear vision, a clear "ask," and the unapologetic practice of asking people to give money to the congregation.

1. Loren Mead, *Financial Meltdown in the Mainline?* (Bethesda: Alban, 1998), 103.

Chapter 1. Money in American Culture

1. Robert Wuthnow, "A Good Life and a Good Society," in Robert Wuthnow, ed., *Rethinking Materialism: Perspectives on the Spiritual Dimension of Economic Behavior* (Grand Rapids: Eerdmans, 1995), 1–21.

2. North American Association of State and Provincial Lotteries, FY99 & FY00 Sales and Profits, *www.naspl.org/9900sale.html*

3. E. Digby Baltzell, *The Protestant Establishment: Aristocracy and Caste in America* (New York: Random House, 1964). Baltzell expressed both his hope for the broadening of the American establishment and his fear that it would protect its homogeneity and privilege at the expense of its leadership role.

4. Wilfred M. McClay, "Where Have We Come Since the 1950s?" in Wuthnow, ed., *Rethinking Materialism*, 29.

5. U.S. Bureau of Economic Analysis (USBEA), National Income and Product Accounts Tables, Table 8.7, "Selected Per Capita Product and Income Series in Current and Chained Dollars," *www.bea.doc.gov/bea/dn/nipaweb*

6. USBEA, Table 1.6, "Relation of Real Gross Domestic Product, Real Gross Domestic Purchases, and Real Final Sales to Domestic Purchasers," *www.bea.doc.gov/bea/dn/nipaweb*

7. John L. Ronsvalle and Sylvia Ronsvalle, *The State of Church Giving*

through 1997 (Champaign, Ill.: Empty Tomb, 1997), 37. The Ronsvalles' data are from a study of 11 Protestant denominations whose statistics were listed in the National Council of Churches-sponsored *Yearbook of American and Canadian Churches*, Eileen Lindner, ed. (Nashville: Abingdon, published annually).

8. Ronsvalle and Ronsvalle, *State of Church Giving*, 8.

9. Larry R. Moran and Clinton McCully, Trends in Consumer Spending, 1959–2000, *Survey of Current Business*, March 2001, 16–21.

10. U.S. Census Bureau, Table IE-1, "Selected Measures of Household Income Dispersion: 1967 to 2000," *www.census.gov/hhes/income/histinc/ ie1.html*

11. Cait Murphy, "Are the rich cleaning up?" *Fortune*, Sept. 4, 2000.

12. Barbara Ehrenreich, *Nickel and Dimed: On (Not) Getting By in America* (New York: Metropolitan Books, 2001), 193–201.

13. Michael Toms, *Money, Money, Money: The Search for Wealth and the Pursuit of Happiness* (Carlsbad, Calif.: New Dimensions Foundation, 1998), 6.

14. Robert Wuthnow, "Pious Materialism: How Americans View Faith and Money," *Christian Century*, March 3, 1993, 239–242.

15. Alexis de Tocqueville, *Democracy in America*, part 1, chapter 3, Henry Reeve, trans., Phillips Bradley, ed. (New York: Alfred A. Knopf, 1945), vol. 1, 53.

16. 2 Cor. 8:15. Paul is quoting Exod. 16:18.

17. Bureau of Labor Statistics, "Labor Productivity and Costs Table," *www.bls.gov/lpc* (Nov. 18, 2001).

18. Juliet B. Schor, *The Overworked American: The Unexpected Decline of Leisure* (New York: Basic Books, 1992), 29–32.

19. Wuthnow, "Pious Materialism," 239–242. See also Robert Wuthnow, *Poor Richard's Principle: Recovering the American Dream through the Moral Dimension of Work, Business, and Money* (Princeton, N.J.: Princeton University Press, 1996), 20–24; 377, n. 8.

20. Schor, *Overworked American*, 128–132.

21. Paraphrased in "Wealth, Torah, and Morality," *Tikkun*, 9:1 (Jan.– Feb. 1994), 57.

22. Mark 10:17-31, "Go, sell everything you have"; Luke 21:3-4, the widow's mite.

23. Matt. 25:14-29.

24. Sondra Ely Wheeler, *Wealth as Peril and Obligation: The New Testament on Possessions* (Grand Rapids: Eerdmans, 1995), 134.

25. Wuthnow, *God and Mammon in America* (New York: MacMillan, 1994), 26.

26. National Highway Traffic Safety Bureau, *Traffic Safety Facts 1999*, 15, table 2. Thanks largely to seat belts and airbags, the fatality rate has declined substantially since peaking at 54,589 in 1972.

27. Exod. 22:25. Seyyed Hossein Nasr, *Ideals and Realities of Islam* (Boston: Beacon, 1972), 108.

28. "Usury," in F. L. Cross, *The Oxford Dictionary of the Christian Church* (Oxford University Press, 1974), 1420.

29. Wuthnow, God and Mammon, 233.

Chapter 2. A Quick Sketch of Your Personal Finances

1. Joe Dominguez and Vicki Robin, *Your Money or Your Life: Transforming Your Relationship with Money and Achieving Financial Independence* (New York: Penguin, 1992, rev. ed., 1999), 31.

2. Edward N. Wolff, *Recent Trends in Wealth Ownership*, 1983–1998, Working Paper No. 300, Levy Economics Institute of Bard College, table 1, available at *www.levy.org*

3. These percentages are pure hokum.

4. The annual percentage rate is correct if you pay off your balance after just one interest-paying month. It actually understates the interest rate on a credit card if you leave a balance due longer than that, because it is simply the monthly rate times 12. A credit card with an APR of 18 percent charges 1.5 percent every month. But after the first month, it charges interest on the interest, so in a year's time you actually will have paid something more like 19.6 percent.

5. Ibbotson Associates of Chicago publish this kind of information in their annual *Stocks, Bonds, Bills, and Inflation* reference books.

Chapter 3. Money as a Spiritual Challenge

1. Robert Wuthnow, "Pious Materialism: How Americans View Faith and Money," *Christian Century*, March 3, 1993, 239–242.

2. Gen. 1.

3. Deut. 8:7-10.

4. Deut. 8:17-18. I have followed the Revised English Bible in verse 17, "yourselves." The NRSV has "yourself," which is consistent with the Pentateuch's general pattern of referring to a patriarchal leader and his clan in the singular but, I think, misleading to the modern reader.

5. Deut. 9:6.

6. Amos 2:6-7.

7. Carol Johnston, "Thinking Theologically about Wealth, Including Money," from the Web site "Resources for American Christianity," *www.resourcingchristianity.org.*

8. Bava Batra 175b.

9. Matt. 19:16-30 and parallels.

10. Luke 19:1-10 and parallels.

11. Mark 14:3-9 and parallels.

12. Wheeler, *Wealth as Peril*, 137.

13. Tocqueville, *Democracy*, part 2, chapter 9, 135.

14. John R. Wimmer, "Symbols of Success: Russell H. Conwell and the Transformation of American Protestantism" (Ph.D. dissertation, University of Chicago, 1992), vol. 1, "Introduction," n.p. The quotation is from Conwell's oft-repeated lecture "Acres of Diamonds," which is available at many sites on the World Wide Web.

15. Ralph Waldo Trine, *In Tune with the Infinite: Fullness of Peace, Power, and Plenty* (New York: Thomas Y. Crowell, 1897), 13, 176.

16. Norman Vincent Peale, *The Power of Positive Thinking* (New York: Prentice-Hall, 1952).

17. 1 Thess. 5:21.

18. Barry Johnson, *Polarity Management: Identifying and Managing Unsolvable Problems* (Amherst, Mass.: HRD Press, [1992] 1996), xvii. "Polarity Management" is a trademark of Polarity Management Associates LLC.

19. Henry David Thoreau, *Walden: Or, Life in the Woods* (Boston: Ticknor & Fields, 1854; reprint, New York: Dover Publications, 1995), 34.

20. Thoreau, *Walden*, 46.

21. Eccles. 3:1, 9-13.

22. Stephen Nissenbaum, *The Battle for Christmas* (New York: Vintage Books, 1996), 6–7.

23. A. L. Basham, *The Wonder That Was India: A Survey of the Culture of the Indian Sub-continent before the Coming of the Muslims* (New York: Grove Press, 1954), 235.

24. Levit. 1:1-17; 6:11-18. *The New Interpreter's Bible* (Nashville: Abingdon, 1994), vol. 1, 1024–1025.

25. Deut. 14:22-29; 26:12-15.

26. James Hudnut-Beumler, *Generous Saints: Congregations Rethinking Ethics and Money* (Bethesda: Alban, 1999), 54.

27. Also known as the parable of the talents: Matt. 25:14-30; Luke 19:11-27. There is a parable of a dishonest steward as well, at Luke 16:1-13.

28. Robert Wood Lynn, "Why Give?" in Mark Chaves and Sharon Miller, eds., *Financing American Religion* (Walnut Creek, Calif.: AltaMira Press, 1999), 59–60.

29. Wuthnow, *God and Mammon*, 143.

30. Peter Block, *Stewardship: Choosing Service over Self-Interest* (San Francisco: Berrett-Koehler, 1993), xx.

31. Wuthnow, *God and Mammon*, 144.

32. Gen. 1:28.

33. Exod. 16.

34. Matt. 14:13-21, and parallels.

35. Matt. 6:25-34.

36. Thorstein Veblen, *The Theory of the Leisure Class: An Economic Study of Institutions* (New York: MacMillan, 1899; reprint New York: New American Library, 1953), 64, 77.

37. Laurie Simon Bagwell and B. Douglas Bernheim, "Veblen Effects in a Theory of Conspicuous Consumption," *American Economic Review* 86 (June 1996).

38. Laurence Shames, *The Hunger for More: Searching for Values in an Age of Greed*, excerpted in *Sales and Marketing Management* 141 (Oct. 1989), 106.

39. Srully Blotnick, "Fit for a King: How to Act Rich, Even Though It May Harm You," *Forbes* 132 (fall 1983), 2.

40. Wuthnow, *God and Mammon*, 155.

41. Wuthnow, *God and Mammon*, 134–6.

42. Thomas J. Stanley and William D. Danko, *The Millionaire Next Door: The Surprising Secrets of America's Wealthy* (New York: Pocket Books, 1996), 32.

43. Wuthnow, *God and Mammon*, 129. "Money is the root of all evil" is a common misquotation of St. Paul's "The love of money . . ." (1 Tim. 6:10).

44. Sharon L. Miller, "The Meaning of Religious Giving," in Chaves and Miller, eds., *Financing American Religion*, 43.

Chapter 4. Congregations Considered Economically

1. With apologies to my Jewish readers, I sneak in here my word "churchcraft," which I propose as a gender-neutral substitute for the old, useful, but now unusable word "churchmanship."

2. Today there are exceptions to this rule, as to virtually all immunities from suit.

3. William S. Gilbert, *Utopia Limited*, Act I.

4. There is no legal requirement that a congregation be incorporated, and many congregations are not. However, most do incorporate when they need to own real estate, employ staff, or accumulate large capital funds. Every state has its own corporation laws, and some treat congregations separately from other nonprofits. However, the broad generalizations offered still apply.

5. Again, a congregational trustee's immunity from suit is not absolute; exceptions vary from state to state, and the trend is toward more, rather than less, exposure.

6. Richard R. Hammar, *Church Law and Tax Report: Church and Clergy Tax Guide*, 2000 edition (Matthews, N.C.: Christian Ministry Resources), 404–405.

7. I am using 5 percent in these examples because it is a good rough estimate of how much you can "draw" from an endowment every year without eroding its value.

8. Cf. Peter F. Drucker, *Managing the Non-Profit Organization: Principles and Practices* (New York: HarperCollins, 1990; reprint HarperBusiness, 1992), xiv–xv.

9. A planning process I have used with congregations that begins from this premise and applies business concepts in a useful way is described in Gary J. Stern, *The Drucker Foundation Self-Assessment Tool: Process Guide*, 2nd ed. (San Francisco: Jossey-Bass, 1999).

10. Ralph Waldo Emerson, "Self-Reliance" (Boston: 1841), in Nina Baym et al., eds., *The Norton Anthology of American Literature*, 2nd ed. (New York: W.W. Norton, 1979), 891–893.

Chapter 5. Advocating for Truthfulness

1. Gary Belsky and Thomas Gilovich, *Why Smart People Make Big Money Mistakes—and How to Correct Them: Lessons from the New Science of Behavioral Economics* (New York: Simon & Schuster, 1999), 65–69.

2. Here is the procedure: Enter the raw giving numbers, year by year, in one column. Put the consumer price index for each year in a column next to them. You can get the CPI at the Web site of the Bureau of Labor Statistics, *www.bli.gov/cpi*. Create a third column, which is the product of the first two, divided by 100. That will give you the "real dollar" amount, pegged to the value of the dollar in the year for which the CPI was arbitrarily set at 100.

3. Actually many people besides clergy get tax-free housing: military personnel, lighthouse keepers, college presidents, astronauts on space stations, and the president of the United States. The broad principle is valid. People who are required to live in certain housing as a condition of employment should not have to treat it as income. Where clergy (and the military) are special is that they are allowed a tax-free housing allowance even if they have wide discretion in choosing and owning homes.

4. As noted in chapter 2, clergy can exempt themselves from paying self-employment tax if they object on conscience to receiving social security benefits. Read carefully: you have to object to the *benefits*, not the tax.

5. Some congregations subtract half of the clergyperson's self-employment tax from the salary shown in the budget, and lump that amount with the employer's share of social security taxes elsewhere in the statement. This makes sense in itself, but seems to me a little disingenuous when nothing is done to correct for the tax benefit of the housing allowance.

Chapter 6. Advocating for Fairness

1. Veblen, *Theory of the Leisure Class*, 206.

2. Matthew J. Price, "Fear of Falling: Male Clergy in Economic Crisis," *Christian Century*, Aug. 15–22, 2001, 18.

3. Charles Merrill Smith, *How to Become a Bishop without Being Religious* (New York: Doubleday, 1965), 91.

Chapter 7. Advocating for Generosity

1. A terminological note: some churches distinguish "fund raising" from "stewardship," and most synagogues distinguish "fund raising" from "dues." I am using the term the way secular fund-raising professionals do, to mean the institution's total strategy for acquiring revenues to support its program. Primarily this means securing charitable gifts from individuals, but it includes special events, dues, fees for service, foundation grants, endowment management, business ventures such as thrift shops, and the

rental of real estate. A congregation's fund-raising strategy needs to include principles for dealing with choices and tradeoffs among these options.

2. Dean Hoge, et al., "Giving in Five Denominations," in Chaves and Miller, *Financing American Religion*, 3.

3. An up-to-date discussion of *tzedakah* is found in Lawrence Bush and Jeffrey Detko, *Jews, Money, and Social Responsibility: Developing a "Torah of Money" for Contemporary Life* (Philadelphia: Shefa Fund, 1993), 113–147.

4. Dean Hoge, ed., *Review of Religious Research*, 36:2. Lay versions of this research are accessible elsewhere: Dean Hoge et al., *Money Matters: Personal Giving in American Churches* (Louisville: Westminster John Knox, 1996), and Hoge et al., "Giving in Five Denominations." My interpretation of the results differs in some respects from theirs, and is informed by data from other sources.

5. Exod. 30:11-16; 35:4-19. I am indebted to Shawn Zevit's wonderful curriculum *A Torah of Money: Jewish Values-Based Approaches to Human and Financial Resources* (Philadelphia: Jewish Reconstructionist Federation, 2000) for highlighting these passages, and for other insights into Jewish thinking about congregational support. The federation's Web site is *www.jrf.org*

6. Dean Hoge, Patrick McNamara, and Charles Zech, *Plain Talk about Churches and Money* (Bethesda: Alban, 1997), 18–19.

7. Lynn, "Why Give?" 59–60.

8. Laurence R. Iannaccone, "Skewness Explained," in Chaves and Miller, *Financing American Religion*, 30.

9. A more nuanced and scientific typology is given in Hoge et al., *Money Matters*, chapter 6, "Motivation and Theology."

Welcome to the work of Alban Institute...
the leading publisher and congregational
resource organization for clergy and laity today.

Your purchase of this book means you have an interest in the kinds of information, research, consulting, networking opportunities and educational seminars that Alban Institute produces and provides. We are a non-denominational, non-profit 25-year-old membership organization dedicated to providing practical and useful support to religious congregations and those who participate in and lead them.

Alban is acknowledged as a pioneer in learning and teaching on *Conflict Management *Faith and Money *Congregational Growth and Change *Leadership Development *Mission and Planning *Clergy Recruitment and Training *Clergy Support, Self-Care and Transition *Spirituality and Faith Development *Congregational Security.

Our membership is comprised of over 8,000 clergy, lay leaders, congregations and institutions who benefit from:
❖ 15% discount on hundreds of Alban books
❖ $50 per-course tuition discount on education seminars
❖ Subscription to *Congregations*, the Alban journal (a $30 value)
❖ Access to Alban research and (soon) the "Members-Only" archival section of our web site www.alban.org

For more information on Alban membership or to be added to our catalog mailing list, call 1-800-486-1318, ext.243 or return this form.

Name and Title: _____

Congregation/Organization: _____

Address: _____

City: _____ Tel.: _____

State: _____ Zip: _____ Email: _____

BKIN

The Alban Institute
Attn: Membership Dept.
7315 Wisconsin Avenue
Suite 1250 West
Bethesda, MD 20814-3211